QUALITY CONTROL IN THE CLINICAL LABORATORY:
A Procedural Text

MICROBIOLOGY
CHEMISTRY
IMMUNOLOGY
URINALYSIS
HEMATOLOGY
CYTOTECHNOLOGY
MATERIALS
TECHNOLOGISTS
PROFICIENCY TESTS
MAINTENANCE
STATISTICS
STANDARDS
NURSES
CONTROLS
PHYSICIANS
PATIENT

QUALITY CONTROL IN THE CLINICAL LABORATORY:
A Procedural Text

by
Paul J. Ottaviano, M.S.

Assistant to the Chief: Technical
Bureau of Laboratories
South Carolina Department of Health and Environmental Control
Columbia, South Carolina

and
Arthur F. DiSalvo, M.D.

Chief, Bureau of Laboratories
South Carolina Department of Health and Environmental Control
Columbia, South Carolina

UNIVERSITY PARK PRESS

Baltimore · London · Tokyo

UNIVERSITY PARK PRESS
International Publishers in Science and Medicine
233 East Redwood Street
Baltimore, Maryland 21202

Copyright © 1977 by University Park Press

Typeset by The Composing Room of Michigan, Inc.
Manufactured in the United States of American by Universal Lithographers, Inc., and The Optic Bindery Incorporated

Library of Congress Cataloging in Publication Data

Ottaviano, Paul J
  Quality control in the clinical laboratory: a procedural text.

  Bibliography: p.
  Includes index.
  1. Medical laboratories—Quality control.
I. DiSalvo, Arthur F., joint author. II. Title.
[DNLM: 1. Quality control. 2. Laboratories—Standards.
3. Technology, Medical—Standards. QY23 089p]
RB36.O88   616.07'5   77-22728
ISBN 0-8391-1156-8

Contents

Figures

Tables

Preface

The purpose of this text is to provide a step-by-step procedure for establishing a program that will meet the minimal requirements for satisfactory quality control as required by the College of American Pathologists, the Joint Commission on Accreditation of Hospitals, and the Clinical Laboratory Improvement Act of 1967, as administered by the Center for Disease Control. At the time of this writing, the requirements of the pending Clinical Laboratory Improvement Act of 1977 also were considered. If a more comprehensive program is desired, the reader should consult the references at the end of this book.

This book was developed from responses to individual requests directed to the South Carolina State Public Health Laboratory for information regarding quality control. Subsequently, as requests for assistance increased, the information was expanded and resulted in this publication. At each stage of development, the primary emphasis has been to make this book a procedural manual for most disciplines in a clinical laboratory.

The authors have accepted the fact that internal quality control and external quality control (proficiency testing) are essential components of competent laboratory performance. Basic concepts have been adapted from the scientific literature and arranged in a practical manner so that any competent laboratorian can institute an acceptable quality control program. Such a program will increase the operating costs of a laboratory, but these costs should be considered no different from the necessary expenditures for equipment, reagents, or supplies.

The 1976 Amendment to the Food and Cosmetic Act (Sections 510–521) will set requirements for the manufacturer regarding medical devices, including media, reagents, and equipment. This will not eliminate the need for user quality control. Unlike the approval of drugs, each product will not be tested. Only those products that do not meet the established performance levels will be brought to the attention of the Food and Drug Administration.

Laboratories that purchase prepared media or reagents should not be lured into false security by depending on the quality control performed by the manufacturer. Even a product prepared under ideal conditions may be subjected to deleterious conditions during shipment or storage by the manufacturer, distributor, or user.

Many laboratorians who are not acquainted with quality control are overwhelmed by the prospect of instituting such a program. It has been our experience that a quality control program is easier to establish if one person is given the responsibility of initiating the procedures for the whole laboratory. The quality control officer should work closely with each supervisor to establish procedures that meet the appropriate licensing criteria and that are compatible with the workload, the facilities, and the personnel. When the program is established, the supervisor then should be given major responsibility for the quality control in his/her area of responsibility.

Brand names and manufacturers are used for identification purposes only and do not constitute an endorsement by the authors or their institution.

Acknowledgments

The authors wish to thank Anne R. Yobs, M.D. (Clinical Chemistry), Leanor D. Haley, Ph.D. (Mycology), Charles T. Hall, Ph.D. (Bacteriology), and George R. Healy, Ph.D. (Parasitology) of the Center for Disease Control, Atlanta, Georgia for reviewing portions of this book. All personnel of the Bureau of Laboratories, South Carolina Department of Health and Environmental Control, Columbia, South Carolina contributed to the quality control program in this laboratory and, therefore, to the experience that led to the writing of this book. Appreciation also is extended to them.

QUALITY CONTROL IN THE CLINICAL LABORATORY:
A Procedural Text

chapter one Why Quality Control?

WHEN DID QUALITY CONTROL BEGIN AND WHERE IS IT NOW?

Perhaps quality control began in the thirteenth century when man's success as a craftsman depended to a large extent on the quality of his product. Methods used at that time probably were limited to visual inspections made as work progressed.

Statistical methods appeared on the scene during the seventeenth century (1). Statistical application was employed first in astronomy and physics, and then later in the biological sciences. In the nineteenth century, de Moivre, LaPlace, and Gauss separately developed a mathematical displacement distribution, which is commonly referred to as the Gaussian Curve. The curve represents the distribution of values from the true value (mean). This mathematical concept is used widely today and is referred to as the "Law of Errors."

Statistics were first applied to quality control during the early part of the twentieth century. In 1924, Walter A. Shewhart of the Bell Telephone Laboratories developed a technique for utilizing charts to evaluate the quality of the product (2). This chart, referred to as the Shewhart Chart, is used in industry and clinical laboratories to document precision of test results. Shewhart was joined later by Dodge and Romig, and the conclusion of their work constitutes the basis of statistical control (3).

Attitudes toward quality control were less than enthusiastic in the early part of the twentieth century. With the advent of World War II, however, the Armed Forces influenced the adoption of sampling inspection techniques in industry.

Clinical laboratories lagged far behind industry in the adoption of quality control techniques. The first publications indicating a need for control procedures in the clinical laboratory did not appear in the literature until 1953 (4).

Today, many laboratories continue to be slow in adopting quality control measures, and a lack of adequate control procedures continues to prevail. The Bureau of Health Insurance and the Bureau of Quality Assurance of the Department of Health, Education and Welfare conducted

1

a survey in March of 1976. Of the 200 laboratories surveyed, citations were as follows: 17% for improper specimen collection; 39% for failure to review and document methodologies annually; 18% for quality control inadequacies in microbiology; 34% for quality control inadequacies in virology; and 34% for failure to include standards, controls, and calibrators, and for failure to calculate and document precision and accuracy.

Federal, state, and professional organizations have, for some time now, been focusing their attention on substandard performance in all phases of clinical laboratories. The role of these organizations is to aid laboratories in such a way as to enable them to institute meaningful and reliable quality control measures. (For a comprehensive review of state and federal regulations, refer to reference 5.)

OUR ULTIMATE RESPONSIBILITY

Before attempting to institute a quality control program, all individuals involved in the formulation and, eventually, the practical application of the program must be aware of their basic mission. Every member of the laboratory group is ultimately responsible for providing the physician with reliable information to assist him in the detection and diagnosis of disease. Automation and diagnostic kits have made it possible for the smallest laboratory to undertake complicated procedures. The laboratory has reached a high degree of refinement in its technological abilities, and this refinement influences the judgment of the physician (6).

One of the basic purposes of quality control is to measure, calculate, predict, and control the variation inherent in any laboratory procedure. Once one is able to predict variation, the allowable limits of variation for any test can be set, and the analyst can ensure the reliability of the data that are generated. Keep in mind that our *ultimate* responsibility is not to ourselves or to our laboratory but rather to the patient who will benefit from our labor.

chapter two

Some General Thoughts Concerning External Quality Control

Quality surveillance programs must be designed to blend with the normal flow of operations in the laboratory. What may be the best method of surveillance in one laboratory may well be impractical in another. Each laboratory responds to somewhat different environments, personnel requirements, continuity of work flow, and test requirements.

For this reason, this manual should be used as a guide from which the reader can establish a quality surveillance program to fulfill the requirements of his/her own laboratory. In a large laboratory with a large staff, this guide should be expanded. In a small laboratory with very few personnel, certain suggestions in this text may not be feasible.

Regardless of the size of the laboratory, however, the analyst must consider the following subjects in his approach to the formulation and institution of a quality surveillance program: 1) specimen condition, 2) procedures, 3) equipment, 4) reagents, chemicals, and media, 5) standards and controls, 6) documentation, 7) feedback systems for remedial action, and 8) personnel proficiency.

These factors can be the causes of variations that will affect the end result. Therefore, for every discipline in the laboratory, they must be controlled by some method.

For brevity, only one remark, with which the reader may be familiar, will be made concerning specimen condition. The end result will only be as precise and accurate as the quality of the specimen received. Specific requirements for specimen condition are well documented; the authors refer the readers to texts for clinical diagnosis (7, 8). It is assumed that the analyst is using the most practical procedure available, i.e., one that is reliable, specific, sensitive, and yet practical in terms of the technician's and the patient's time and money. The precision and accuracy of the procedure can be determined as described on pp. 17–30.

With the exception of this chapter, the remainder of the text is concerned with factors 3 through 7 as they apply to specific areas in the clinical laboratory. The techniques described in this text represent a review of the literature as well as the quality surveillance techniques used in the various sections of the authors' laboratory. The use of trade names or referenced procedures is not to be taken as an endorsement by the authors or their laboratory.

Judicious use of this text, together with those regulations to which your laboratory may be subject (Medicare, College of American Pathologists, State and Federal Licensure), will ensure that a high degree of accuracy and precision is generated by your laboratory. Recall the introductory remark that our ultimate concern is not to satisfy requirements, but to ensure the reliability of the information reported to the physician. We should be promoters of better patient care, and better patient care is our professional responsibility.

The laboratory director must instill in each technician a sense of the importance of strict adherence to the steps set down in the laboratory procedures manual. The technician must be made aware of the serious consequences of unauthorized procedural modifications or shortcuts in techniques. The procedures manual itself should conform to the guidelines set forth in the Clinical Laboratory Improvement Act. The laboratory director must keep the staff informed concerning the purpose and implementation of quality control programs and this information and training must be extended to the evening and night staff as well.

Participation in out-of-house proficiency testing (external quality control) also is essential. It is the authors' opinion, however, that out-of-house proficiency tests usually result in the collusion of two or more parties. This adds an intolerable degree of bias to the test. While the out-of-house proficiency tests offered by many state, federal, and private agencies have the ability to point out gross errors, the day-to-day methods and treatments which a routine sample receives usually are not brought to the surface through this type of proficiency testing, simply because everyone realizes that it is a test specimen. It is only human nature to want to do one's best on an examination that will be subjected to the supervisor's scrutiny.

How can the laboratory director test the functioning of his/her system as a whole and expect to receive a realistic picture of the precision and accuracy in his/her laboratory? Our answer: Introduce spiked samples into the normal flow of work. Sera saved from a previous proficiency test may be used for this purpose. The director is aware of the contents of the submitted material because he/she may have prepared it. The director should channel the specimen to each technician on a routine basis, and the report should be allowed to go back to the ward of origin before it is collected and reviewed. This will serve to check clerical help and data handling systems. The obvious value of this type of check system is that the spiked specimen is treated routinely. You may be surprised, one way or the other, when you receive the results. Problem areas can be pinpointed and corrected immediately.

The sender is often blamed for inadequate specimens received by the laboratory. To alleviate this problem, it may be advantageous to prepare and distribute to all personnel involved in the requisition of laboratory examinations a guide to laboratory services. The guide should contain detailed instructions including:

1. hours of operation of the laboratory
2. list of tests performed on a routine basis by section and a brief description of the interpretation of results
3. available laboratory supplies
4. proper procedures for requesting specimen analysis
5. type and quantity of material required
6. emergency laboratory service
7. collection, preservation, and storage before the delivery of specimens
8. color key for vacuum tubes
9. key personnel to be contacted when necessary

chapter three

Control of Incoming Materials

CONTROL OF INCOMING REAGENTS, CHEMICALS, AND MEDIA

The reagents, chemicals, and media purchased by a laboratory have already undergone some type of quality control checks before their release from the manufacturer. This well known fact lures some analysts into a false sense of security with regard to the products they use. While quality control is performed on the materials before they are released by the manufacturer, many factors may affect the product in such a manner as to cause deterioration while in the warehouse, during transit, or on the shelves of the laboratory stockroom. With this in mind, the analyst is obligated to ensure that before its use in a test the product will perform as stated.

Purchase Orders

Purchase orders received by the manufacturer can be thought of as an instruction. The purchase order, among other things, implies that the manufacturer is to label containers and packing slips with the following information: name of the material, manufacturer's name, lot number, expiration date, quantity, material specification number, and date. Copies of all purchase orders should be kept on file and reviewed by the administrative personnel to make certain that the most up-to-date requirements for materials are being met.

Incoming Material

The laboratory supply officer should sort incoming reagents, chemicals, and media and check the package markings against the copies of the purchase order. This will prevent unacceptable materials from ever reaching the analyst and being used in the test. If the material is accepted by the supply officer, a record similar to the following should be kept:

RECEIVING LOG

Identification	Manufacturer	Date	P.O. Number	Expiration Date

The shelf-life expiration date should be stamped on the container at the factory. A small label should be placed on the container upon receipt with the following notations: 1) date received, 2) date opened (to be filled in by the analyst), and 3) expiration date, if any. This will prevent materials with a limited shelf-life from being used past their dates of expiration.

In addition, laboratory personnel should survey the inventory once a month to identify and reorder materials approaching expiration date. This inventory also will enable the technologist to set up a reorder point on all materials based on usage rates and, thereby, will prevent stock depletion (9). Finally, it is advisable to check the strength, concentration, and composition of reagents, solutions, solvents, media, etc., against standards before use in an analysis. Records of the "blanks," as they might be termed, should be kept on file with other pertinent quality control records.

Each reagent and solution must be properly labeled to include: identity, titer, strength or concentration, storage requirements, preparer, date of preparation, date of expiration, and hazards.

chapter four Equipment Maintenance

PREVENTIVE MAINTENANCE

A well planned preventive maintenance program of periodic inspection usually results in minor adjustments or repairs. The cost of this type of inspection is insignificant when compared to the inoperative time and cost incurred through the loss of revenue and the expensive repairs that seem to go hand-in-hand with a major breakdown.

Industry keeps major repairs to a minimum and consequently reduces operating cost figures on financial statements by *periodic preventive maintenance*. The same techniques used in industry can be applied to the clinical laboratory. Suggestions for initiating the program include:

1. Establishment of files, to include service manuals, specifications, and warranties. These manuals should give the schedule and types of maintenance that will be performed on the instruments, and they may be used to start your system.
2. Service Contracts. Acceptance or rejection of a service contract on an instrument will depend on the competence of instrument specialists on your staff. A well trained instrumentation specialist providing periodic maintenance evaluations will keep breakdowns to a minimum. In this case, out-of-house service would be most economically performed on a noncontract basis.
3. Development of a list of inspection points and frequencies of inspection and maintenance (Table 1). From this list, create individual records for each instrument. The record should be kept on the instrument, and a copy should be filed with the individual responsible for maintenance. The record should include the following information: 1) name, serial number, date of purchase, and initial cost, 2) points to be checked, 3) frequency of the check, 4) record performance parameters, 5) record of changes made to restore accuracy and precision, 6) cost associated with restoration (parts), and 7) time spent on restoration (inspector's time and cost).

Table 1. Preventive maintenance record

Date	Instrument	Maintenance	Initial of technician
2/1/75	Microhematocrit centrifuge (0−11−23)	Oiled bearings, replaced gasket	R. Brower
3/17/75	Autoanalyzer (5−61−01)	Replaced all coils, cleaned pump	R. Brower
7/16/75	Coleman II (4−50−11)	Replaced photoelectric cell	B. Horne

CALIBRATION AND CONFIRMATION OF EQUIPMENT

Calibration is defined as a quantitative measurement of the instrument undertaken to ensure accurate performance. *Confirmation* is defined as steps taken to ensure the proper operation of an instrument. Calibration applies to instruments such as pH meters, spectrophotometers, and auto-analyzers, while confirmation applies to water bath temperatures, incubator temperatures, centrifuge speeds, and so forth. Confirmation is useful only at the point in time when it is determined. Examples:

1. pH Meter. Calibrate daily using a series of known buffers. Keep a record of the results.
2. Spectrophotometers. Confirm the *wavelength* daily, using a didymium filter, and calibrate using a standard solution with a known absorbance on a monthly basis (linearity check), or whenever new lots of controls, reagents, or standards are obtained.
3. Analytical balances. Daily or weekly, depending on use, calibrate with a set of Class S weights purchased from a scientific supplier and certified by the National Bureau of Standards (NBS).
4. Volumetric equipment. All pipettes and autodiluters should be routinely checked for volume of delivery. Ideally this should be accomplished each day of use by delivering multiple volumes into a Class A volumetric flask (To Contain). For example, to determine the volume of delivery of a 10.0 ml autodiluter, use a 50.0 ml Class A volumetric flask (T.C.). Depress the autodiluter five times. The level of fluid in the filled flask should be exactly at the 50.0 ml line.
5. Refrigerators and freezers. In large chest-type freezers, walk-in freezers, or walk-in refrigerators, a recording thermometer should be installed. In upright refrigerators and freezers, calibrated thermometers immersed in water (for refrigerators) or alcohol (for freezers) should be installed.
6. Water baths. The most common problem is an uneven, fluctuating temperature caused by improper maintenance of water level, a faulty thermostat, or poor design. The temperature should be checked twice a day with an adequate, precalibrated thermometer. The temperature should be checked at more than one location to exclude the possibility of hot or cold spots.
7. Thermometers. All thermometers used in the laboratory must be checked routinely against a certified National Bureau of Standards (NBS) precision thermometer, accurate to within one division. The thermometers should be checked over the entire range of tempera-

Table 2. Recommended preventive maintenance (PM) check points and frequencies of inspection

Item of equipment	PM inspection points and action required	Frequency of PM
Centrifuge	Lubricate bearings (if not permanently lubricated and sealed)	Quarterly
	Remove head and dust cover and add lubricant so grease cup is kept full	Quarterly
	Check commutator for scratches, grooves, or dirt; use fine sandpaper (0 or 00) if roughened	Quarterly
	Check brushes and replace if worn to 5/16 inch	Quarterly
	Check autotransformer carbon brush and replace if less than 1/16 inch is protruding	Quarterly
	Wash chamber and cover gasket; check for wear or cracks in gasket	Quarterly
	For refrigerated centrifuges, listen for noisy condenser; clean condenser coils of dust and lint, and vacuum or dry brush condenser fins	Semi-annually
	Check oil level in reservoir	Semi-annually
	Check rotor nut and shaft threads	Semi-annually
	Replace grease in grease cup	Annually
Sterilizer (and Autoclave)	Check valves and fittings for leaks; check door gasket for leaks, hardening, and cracking	Monthly
	Clean steam traps and strainers; check for leaks and restrictions	Monthly
	Check operation of steam safety valve, gauges, instruments, lights, timers, recorders	Monthly
	Spray door gaskets with silicone	Semi-annually
	Lubricate drive motors if equipped	Semi-annually
	Lubricate door hinges and locking devices	Semi-annually

Refrigerator and Freezer	Check door hinges and latch for tightness and free operation	Monthly
	Check door gasket for cracks, deterioration, and security of attachment	Monthly
	Check operation of pilot and interior lights	Monthly
	Check evaporator and condensate drain	Monthly
	Check for frost buildup and defroster operation	Monthly
	Check compressor for leaks, corrosion, and proper operation	Monthly
	Check belt tension and oil level on unsealed units	Monthly
	Lubricate door hinges and lock	Semi-annually
	Clean compressor unit and condenser coils	Semi-annually
Incubator	Check operation of all indicator lights and switches	Bi-weekly
	Check for carbon dioxide leaks	Bi-weekly
	Adjust door gaskets if loose; replace if cracked	Quarterly
	Check thermostat against accurate thermometer	Quarterly
	For egg incubators, check humidity and motor and timer-setting for egg turn	Quarterly
Lyophilizer	Check V-belts for wear, tension, and alignment	Monthly
	Check hardware and mounting bolts for tightness	Monthly
	Check oil level in vacuum pump and compressor; check for moisture in oil	Monthly
	Check valve operation and packing	Monthly
	Check door gasket condition; check unit for leaks	Monthly
Oven	Adjust door gaskets if loose; replace if cracked	Semi-annually
	Clean visible heating elements	Semi-annually
	Check cord and plug for brittleness	Semi-annually
	Check thermostat against accurate thermometer	Semi-annually

continued

Table 2.—*Continued*

Item of equipment	PM inspection points and action required	Frequency of PM
pH Meter	Check electrode for loss of sensitivity and change glass or calomel electrode as needed	Weekly
	Rinse electrodes used for blood pH with saline, then water	After each use
	Check input tube, mechanical zero (whenever moved), and water bath	Quarterly
	Clean switch assembly contacts	Annually
Spectrophotometer	Check bulbs for dirt or dust and wipe clean with a cloth	Bi-weekly
	Readjust Xenon lamps	Bi-weekly
	Clean, rinse, and dry cuvettes	Bi-weekly
	Wipe clean exit and collimating mirrors, or wash with alcohol and distilled water and drain dry	Bi-weekly
Flame Photometer	Disassemble and clean manifold or compressor air filter	Monthly
	Clean element from air compressor intake muffler	Quarterly
	Replace air filters that cannot be cleaned	Semi-annually
	Remove and clean chimney	Semi-annually
	Check and clean cooling system	Annually
	Replace cleanable air filters	Annually
	Immediately clean dirt from atomizer bowl	When visibly dirty
	Clean burner head and ignition block of encrusted salts	When salts form

Colorimeter

Wash out entire system .... Daily
Check alignment and cleanliness of flow cells .... Daily
Check cuvettes and clean or discard marred sample holders ... Daily
Check flow cell connections for leaks .... Weekly
Check filters and clean with lens paper if necessary; wipe apertures free
  of dust with damp cloth .... Weekly
Remove colorimeter cover and inspect for spillage ...... Monthly
Inspect and clean lamp .... Monthly
Clean entire optical system, including lenses .... Quarterly
Check flow cell tubing and replace if needed .... Quarterly

Adapted from "A Guide on Laboratory Administration," 1976, U.S. Department of Health, Education and Welfare, Public Health Service, Health Services and Mental Health Administration, Center for Disease Control, Atlanta, Georgia 30333.

tures to be measured by the thermometer. The NBS thermometer can be purchased with instructions for calibration (Fisher Scientific).

8. Ovens and incubators. Overcrowding will restrict the movement of air and cause a difference of temperature between the top and bottom of the instrument. By placing two thermometers in the instrument, one near the top and one near the bottom, the temperature gradient between the upper and lower shelves can be determined. Once a maximal acceptable load has been determined, i.e., an amount that does not cause significant temperature variations, it must not be exceeded. These temperatures must be monitored daily.

9. Autoclaves. Daily inspection of the recording thermometer, coupled with monthly determination of sterilization efficiency using some type of biological indicator such as Killit Ampules, will ensure proper performance of the sterilizer. For more information concerning preventive maintenance of autoclaves, refer to the recommended check list set forth in Table 2.

10. Stills. In addition to daily inspection of the water for pH and conductivity, the still should be cleaned periodically. Cleaning procedures are specified in the instruction manual that comes with the still. Basically, the still is drained, a 3% solution of HCl is used to fill the boiler, and the still is run for 2–3 hours, drained, and flushed with distilled water several times.

(For further information concerning preventive maintenance refer to references 10–12.)

Table 2 provides a partial list of the more common instruments found in a clinical laboratory and outlines their recommended preventive maintenance. The checkpoints and frequencies were adapted from "A Guide on Laboratory Administration" (reference 16) and are used in the authors' laboratory. The reader should expand this list to include each piece of operational equipment in his/her laboratory. The manufacturers' service manuals are an excellent source of information. Additional preventive maintenance procedures are detailed in specific sections of this text.

chapter five

The Basis of Statistical Quality Control

Statistical quality control (SQC) may be employed in the various areas of a clinical laboratory to aid in the measurement, evaluation, and prediction of variation. However, before attempting to apply the laws of statistics to laboratory data, an understanding of the basic concepts of uncertainty and variability is necessary.

CONCEPTS OF UNCERTAINTY AND VARIABILITY

Uncertainty

All measurements are subject to uncertainty because of several factors. The following are some of the outside factors that may affect the clinical result and that therefore must be considered:

1. Patient's physiological variability. Laboratory results are influenced by the patient's age, sex, diet, medications, the time of day, and so forth.
2. Specimen environment. Factors affecting the results in this category include microbiological contamination, chemical contamination, excessive exposure to light, oxidation, pH, loss of CO_2, and temperature variation.
3. Specimen condition. In various analyses, factors such as specimen type, hemolysis, lipemia, bilirubinemia, presence of anticoagulants, and medications may cause variation in the results significant enough to actually be considered hazardous to the patient (13).

Laboratory personnel should be aware of the above variables. The supervisors and laboratory director bear the responsibility of informing the sender of the correct methods for specimen collection and shipment. A Laboratory Services Manual is perhaps the most effective means of conveying the message.

Variability

Gaussian Distribution and Normal Variation   The law of errors tells us that any group of measurements on the same sample, subject, or homogeneous group normally appears clustered about the mean observation. The frequency of the distribution falls about the mean in a somewhat predictable bell-shaped curve often referred to as a Gaussian Distribution (Figure 1). When specimens from a normal, nonbiased population are tested repetitively (30–100 times), the values observed will *vary* within a *given range*. The variation depends on several factors which are discussed later; however, in a usual Gaussian Distribution, one standard deviation (± 1S) will include 68.26% of all the determinations, two standard deviations (± 2S) will include 95.44% of all the determinations, and three standard deviations (± 3S) will include 99.75% of all the determinations. Therefore, one could expect that out of a total of 22 determinations one of them would fall outside the 2S limits, either above or below. This is sometimes referred to as "normal variation" (14). Most experimenters try to control a test at the 2S level.

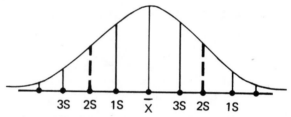

3S 2S 1S   X̄   3S 2S 1S

Figure 1. Gaussian Distribution. The bellshaped curve represents the somewhat predictable distribution of values from the mean.

Central Tendency   There are several measures of central tendency, of which the most frequently used is the arithmetic mean. This is calculated by adding each individual value and dividing by the number of determinations added. The mean (sometimes called the average) is represented by the formula:

$$\overline{X} = \frac{\Sigma X}{n}$$

where, $\overline{X}$ = mean
Σ = sum of
X = observed values
n = number of individual values

Mode Often abbreviated as Mo, the mode is the value that appears most frequently in a series. It is sometimes referred to as the "peak value" of the frequency distribution (13, 15).

Median Value If one arranges the results of all determinations in numerical order, the median value is the middle determination. If there is an even number of items, the average of the middle two items represents the median value.

Dispersion The dispersion (or scatter of results) is usually expressed as the *range* or as the *standard deviation*.

1. Range. The range is simply the difference between the smallest and the largest value in a set of determinations.
2. Standard Deviation. Standard deviation of a representative sample of the population is given by the symbol S. Standard deviation can be calculated for a series of replicate determinations using the formula:

$$S = \sqrt{\frac{\Sigma(\overline{X} - \overline{\overline{X}})^2}{n-1}}$$

where, S = standard deviation, ($\overline{X}$ values about $\overline{\overline{X}}$)
$\overline{X}$ = mean of two analyses of each duplicate or $\overline{X} = \dfrac{(X1 + X2)}{2}$
$\overline{\overline{X}}$ = mean of the means or $\overline{\overline{X}} = \Sigma\overline{X}/n$.
$\Sigma(\overline{X} - \overline{\overline{X}})^2$ = sum of the differences squared
$(n-1)$ = number of determinations minus one degree of freedom

Coefficient of Variation The coefficient of variation (CV) is defined as the sample variability relative to the mean of the sample expressed in percent. CV can be calculated for a particular type of test using the formula:

$$CV = \left[\frac{(S\overline{X})}{\overline{\overline{X}}}\right] 100$$

where, $\overline{\overline{X}}$ = mean of the means
$S\overline{X}$ = one standard deviation $\overline{X}$ values about $\overline{\overline{X}}$

It should be noted that variations also arise from sampling distributions. The smaller the sample size, the greater the variation. It usually is recommended that a sample size of no less than 30 be used when estimating standard deviation with the above.

Population Variability (normal values, critical values, reference values) Almost all assays in the clinical laboratory have a "Normal Range."

Samples from a "healthy person" do not fall above or below this range. These values are determined by sampling a large cross-section of the population and evaluating the test results by sex, age, and past disease history. The following example, which illustrates one instance of population variability, may prove useful as an abbreviated example of how these values are determined. The data in Table 3 were obtained in the authors' laboratory from 30 fasting outpatients with no history of disease. Using these data, make the following calculations:

1. For each patient (at least 30 patients), collect one serum sample, analyze it in duplicate, and record the results.
2. Calculate the range between Trial 1 and Trial 2 for each patient and record under R.
3. Calculate the average value for each trial and record under $\overline{X}$.
4. Determine the average of all $\overline{X}$ by adding the column $\overline{X}$ and divide by n.

$$\frac{\Sigma \overline{X}}{n} = \frac{2,772}{30} = 92.4$$

92.4 is referred to as $\overline{\overline{X}}$ (the mean of all averages).

5. Calculate the difference between $\overline{X}$ for each trial and $\overline{\overline{X}}$ for each patient. Example: Row 1. $\overline{X} - \overline{\overline{X}} = 94.5 - 92.4 = 2.1$
6. Square each value obtained in Step 5. $(\overline{X} - \overline{\overline{X}})^2$
7. Determine the sum of the column. $(\overline{X} - \overline{\overline{X}}) = 2,179.15$
8. Take the square root.

$$\sqrt{\frac{(\overline{X} - \overline{\overline{X}})^2}{n - 1}} = \sqrt{\frac{2,179.15}{30 - 1}} = 8.67$$

One standard deviation (S) = 8.67 (Table 3), page 21. Recall that this means 68.26% of our population can be expected to have test values within ±8.67 of the mean if the population is distributed normally. "Normal values" are calculated based on two standard deviations, however.

By setting the "Normal Limits," using the data and calculations of Table 3, the normal range for this population can be calculated:

1. Scientific procedures are controlled within two standard deviations of the mean.
2. S = 8.67 in our example; therefore, two standard deviations = ±1.96 (S) = 16.99 or −16.99. (Note: Most texts express the value ±1.96 as 2.0 which represents 95.54%. The value ±1.96 represents 95% of the population.)

Table 3. Population variability data

Date of analysis	Trial 1	Trial 2	R	$\overline{X}$	$\overline{X} - \overline{\overline{X}}$	$(\overline{X} - \overline{\overline{X}})^2$
	95	94	1	94.5	2.1	4.41
	97	95	2	96.0	3.6	12.98
	100	102	2	101.0	7.6	57.76
	84	83	1	83.5	8.9	79.21
	83	83	0	83.0	9.4	88.36
	90	94	4	92.0	0.4	0.16
	93	91	2	92.0	0.4	.16
	97	95	2	96.0	3.6	12.96
	103	103	0	103.0	0.6	0.36
	96	94	2	95.0	2.6	6.76
	102	100	2	101.0	8.6	73.96
	97	97	0	97.0	4.6	21.16
	94	91	3	92.5	0.1	0.01
	103	100	3	101.5	9.1	82.81
	97	99	2	98.0	5.6	31.36
	79	76	3	77.5	14.9	222.01
	110	111	1	110.5	18.1	327.61
	102	99	3	100.5	8.1	65.61
	101	100	1	100.5	8.1	65.61
	76	72	4	74.0	18.4	338.56
	83	80	3	81.5	10.9	118.81
	87	90	3	88.5	3.9	15.21
	83	81	2	82.0	10.4	108.16
	85	81	4	83.0	9.4	88.36
	79	76	3	77.5	14.9	222.01
	104	100	4	102.0	9.6	92.16
	86	88	2	87.0	5.4	29.16
	94	92	2	93.0	0.6	0.36
	92	90	2	91.0	1.4	1.96
	96	98	2	97.0	4.6	21.16
Total	30		65	2,772.0		2,179.15

Analysis: Serum glucose by O-Toluidine procedures.

3. The mean $\overline{\overline{X}}$ = 92.4.
4. Normal limits based on our test procedure using 30 patients:

$$
\begin{array}{lcl}
92.4 = \overline{\overline{X}} & & 92.4 = \overline{\overline{X}} \\
\underline{-16.9 = 2\overline{X}S} & \text{to} & \underline{+16.9 = 2\overline{X}S} \\
(75.5 \text{ mg\%} & & 109.3 \text{ mg\%})
\end{array}
$$

This system has taken population variability into account. Figure 2 provides a graphic representation. Without some knowledge of the variability of the population, the data would be of doubtful worth.

Measuring Variability

Analytical Variability: Precision and Accuracy No matter how well controlled a scientific procedure is, it will, by nature, have inherent sources of random or chance variation. As with population variability, the limits of inherent variation must be defined and recognized to prevent situations that could be detrimental to the health and safety of the patient, such as a case in which test results of decreased reliability would be reported.

Relative to a method of testing, *precision* is the degree of mutual agreement among individual measurements made under prescribed-like conditions. Precision of an analytical procedure can be estimated from replicate determinations or reference materials.

Calculating Precision The following represents one of several acceptable practical methods for determining precision in a clinical laboratory: Over a 72-hour period (to include evening and night operation, if applicable) run every tenth patient specimen in duplicate and record the results. After analyzing no less than 30 replicates (preferably 100), calculate upper and lower control limits at the 3S level and upper and lower warning limits at the 2S level as follows:

1. Calculate the average range.

$$
\frac{\Sigma R}{n} = \overline{R}
$$

2. Calculate

$UCL_R = (D_4)(\overline{R})$
LCL_R (same as UCL_R)

(Note: Upper or lower (UCL_R, LCL_R) control limit refers to ± 3 standard deviations. D_4 for Duplicates = 3.27 constant at 99% or 3S level only.)

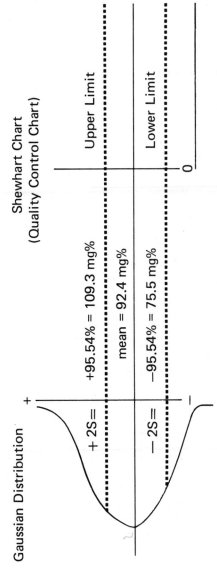

Figure 2. Graphic representation of population variability. Serum glucose analysis by O-Toluidine procedures.

3. Calculate

$$UWL_R = \frac{2}{3}((D_4)(\overline{R}) - \overline{R}) + \overline{R}$$
LWL_R (same as UWL_R)

(Note: Upper or lower (UWL_R, LWL_R) warning limit refers to ±2 standard deviations.)

Table 4 provides an example of precision data. The hypothetical data were obtained from analyses of individual patients run in duplicate. Nitrate was the constituent for which the analysis was made. The minimal detectable limit for the procedure used was 0.1 mg/liter. Calculations are as follows:

1. Calculate $\overline{R}$.

$$\overline{R} = \frac{\Sigma R}{n} = \frac{2.70}{30} = 0.09$$

2. Calculate

UCL_R $= (D_4)(\overline{R})$
           $= (3.27)(0.09) = 0.2943$
LCL_R $= 0$ (because it is impossible to have a negative range)

(Note: D_4 is a constant. For replicate determinations at the 3S level, D_4 is equal to 3.27 (U.S. Environmental Protection Agency, 1972 (June). Manual of Analytical Quality Control. Cincinnati, Ohio (16)).

3. Calculate

UWL_R $= \frac{2}{3}((D_4)(\overline{R}) - \overline{R}) + \overline{R}$
           $= \frac{2}{3}((3.27)(0.09) - (0.09)) + 0.09 = 0.2262$
LWL_R $= 0$

What Do We Do with the Results?

The precision for this particular analysis has been estimated. The operating control limits have also been calculated. For daily use, the analyst now can construct a quality control chart (Shewhart Chart).

Method of Construction   Construction of the Quality Control Chart should be conducted as follows:

1. Select a point on the vertical axis as 0. Zero means no range.

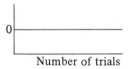

Number of trials

Table 4. Precision data (duplicate analysis of sera for nitrate over a 72-hour period)

	Date	Specimen no.	Trial 1 (mg/liter)	Trial 2 (mg/liter)	Range (mg/liter)
7:00 AM	3/21/74	1	3.00	3.10	0.10
	3/21/74	2	2.19	2.19[a]	0.05
	3/21/74	3	3.00	2.85	0.15
	3/21/74	4	0.90	0.90	0.05
	3/21/74	5	4.70	4.80	0.10
	3/21/74	6	0.76	0.76	0.05
	3/21/74	7	1.97	1.97	0.05
12:00 AM	3/21/74	8	4.10	4.00	0.10
1:00 PM	3/21/74	9	2.37	2.37	0.05
	3/21/74	10	1.02	1.02	0.05
	3/21/74	11	4.20	4.00	0.20
	3/21/74	12	4.60	4.80	0.20
	3/21/74	13	0.97	0.97	0.05
	3/21/74	14	1.45	1.45	0.05
	3/21/74	15	1.23	1.23	0.05
8:00 PM	3/21/74	16	0.95	0.90	0.05
	3/21/74	17	1.10	1.10	0.05
	3/21/74	18	1.16	1.16	0.05
7:00 AM	3/22/74	19	4.30	4.40	0.10
	3/22/74	20	4.47	4.67	0.20
	3/22/74	21	3.00	3.15	0.15
	3/22/74	22	3.10	3.20	0.10
	3/22/74	23	2.15	2.15	0.05
	3/22/74	24	2.12	2.12	0.05
	3/22/74	25	5.60	5.80	0.20
7:00 AM	3/23/74	26	1.96	1.96	0.05
	3/23/74	27	2.15	2.05	0.10
	3/23/74	28	1.67	1.67	0.05
	3/23/74	29	0.90	0.90	0.05
	3/23/74	30	2.45	2.30	0.15
					2.70

[a]If the range is 0, use as the range one-half the minimal detectable limit = 0.05.

2. Plot the calculated UCL.

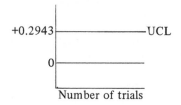

3. Plot the UWL.

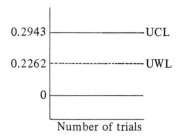

It is recommended that, on a daily basis, the analyst space duplicates randomly within each 10 patients' specimens. As long as the mean and range for any duplicate fall within the established operating control limits, the analyst can assume that the test is in control. Reference materials can also be depicted on the charts. If the range falls outside control limits, variability has increased and then the test procedure should be stopped and corrective measures taken. Trends may occur over a period of time. For instance, laboratory Y noticed its controls and duplicates rising toward the UCL over a three-day period. The problem was reagent deterioration. The use of this method enables the analyst to ensure the reliability of reported results by detecting excess analytical error. Quality control records must be kept for a period of two years for legal purposes.

Some Possible Causes of Control Chart Problems The following outline represents a list of possible problems and their causes that may be detected if the analyst uses control charts. This list was compiled by Dr. Adrian Hainlain, Center for Disease Control.

A. Shift of the mean upward
1. Standard concentration low
  a. Preparation error (underweight) (overdilution)
  b. Deterioration
2. Reagents (standard treated differently from control)
  a. Impurity of stock
  b. Contamination

    c. Preparative error (conditions of analysis may not allow inter-ference)

3. Instruments (standard treated differently from controls)
    a. Incorrect wavelength setting or filter (allows interference)
    b. Incubation temperature or time error
    c. Dilutor or pipettor error
    d. Manifold error or pump tubing fatigue (atomic absorption (AA))

4. Control concentration high
    a. Reconstitution error (underdilution)
    b. Evaporation of a portion of control samples

5. Other
    a. Increase in blank after standards have been run (CPK)

B. Shift of the mean downward

1. Standard concentration high
    a. Preparation error (overweight) (underdilution)
    b. Evaporation

2. Reagents (standard treated differently from controls)
    a. Impurity of stock
    b. Contamination
    c. Preparative error
    d. One of above to produce shift up during control study

3. Instruments (standard treated differently from controls)
    a. Incorrect wavelength setting or filter
    b. Incubation temperature or time error
    c. Dilutor or pipettor error

4. Controls
    a. Reconstitution error
    b. Deterioration of a portion of control samples

C. Trend of the mean upward

1. Standard concentration decreasing
    a. Deterioration
    b. Contamination

2. Reagents (standard treated differently from samples)
    a. Deterioration

3. Instruments (standard treated differently from samples)
    a. Pipettor or dilutor error
    b. Manifold error or pump tubing fatigue (AA)

4. Controls
    a. Evaporation in storage

D. Drift of the mean downward

1. Standard concentration increasing
    a. Evaporation

    2. Reagents (standard treated differently from samples)
       a. Deterioration
    3. Instruments (standard treated differently from samples)
       a. Pipettor or dilutor error
       b. Manifold error or pump tubing fatigue (AA)
    4. Controls
       a. Deterioration in storage
E. Loss in precision
    1. Standard concentration variable
       a. Preparation variability
       b. Evaporation during procedure
       c. Poor mixing
    2. Reagents
       a. Preparation variability
       b. Improper mixing
    3. Instruments
       a. Manifold (AA) (erratic flow, surging, fatigue, damaged)
       b. Erratic pumps
       c. Pipettor or dilutor error
       d. Water bath temperature (erratic)
       e. Erratic photometer electronics (noise)
       f. Inconsistent use
       g. Dirty glassware
    4. Controls
       a. Reconstitution errors (variable technique)
       b. Improper mixing (after thawing or during reconstitution)
    5. Personnel
       a. Technique (improper mixing, pipetting, use of instruments)
       b. Training failure or lack
       c. Improper procedure
    6. Other: Enzyme substrate inadequacy

Accuracy Accuracy is the degree of agreement of individual measurements with an accepted reference value (as determined by reference method). This implies the use of *assayed material.* In biologicals, it is impossible to "know" true value; therefore, one must work with *accepted* values.

Accuracy can be determined by analyzing assayed controls with known amounts of material present or by preparing an accuracy control as follows:

1. Obtain a patient's specimen (normal fasting serum) and repeat the analysis on the serum seven times. Divide the sum of the seven results

Table 5. Accuracy data

	Observed after spike	(Spike = 0.60 units)
	0.105 units	
	0.105	
	0.105	
	0.110	
	0.110	
	0.110	
	0.105	
Average =	0.107	

by seven to obtain the *average* amount of material contained in the specimen (0.059 units in the example, Table 5). The data used to arrive at 0.059 are not shown.

2. Add (spike) the serum with a certified standard to equal the amount of the average. In Table 5, 0.60 units is added. The amount of the standard added to the serum is arbitrary, provided the amount added is known and accurate.

3. Repeat the analysis seven times and take the average of the seven values (0.107 in Table 5).

4. Calculate accuracy (% recovery) as follows (16):

$$A = \frac{(0)}{(Ai + S)} (100)$$

where, A = accuracy expressed as a percent
0 = observed average after spike
Ai = initial observed value before spike
S = amount of standard added to serum
$$A = \frac{(0.107 \text{ units})}{(0.059 \text{ units} + 0.06 \text{ units})} (100) = 90\%$$

The analyst should strive for 95% recovery. Certain tests are considered to be acceptable if 90% accuracy is obtained. Most quality control is precision-control oriented. Maximum accuracy is established when method, instrumentation, etc., are selected for. Accuracy should be determined using assayed controls within each batch of patients' specimens. Remember, precision without regard for accuracy may cause the analyst to be "precisely wrong."

chapter six Quality Control in the Blood Bank

All departments, through consistently incorrect values, can influence a wrong diagnosis or improper treatment. In the area of the blood bank, one incorrect value will rapidly lead to improper treatment, a transfusion reaction, and possible death. This is not to say that quality control is more important in this area than it is in others. However, the lack of relevant control in this area may do harm to the patient in a much shorter span of time than the lack of control and the reporting of incorrect results in any other area of the laboratory. The key distinction lies in the amount of time required to do the harm.

Routine comparison of results on the same specimen should be conducted because of the nature of blood banking. The more obvious areas of concern are reagent titration, antibody identification, crossmatches, grouping, and typing. If the laboratory finds this to be an extreme hardship because of time and talent, then comparisons may be limited solely to problem specimens.

MONITORING REAGENTS

As previously described, much can happen to a reagent to cause deterioration, concentration, and loss of specificity. It remains the sole responsibility of the laboratory to ensure the reliability of the reagents used.

Antiserum Quality Control

Reactivity The Bureau of Biologics' (BOB), Department of Health, Education and Welfare, minimum requirements for antisera are set forth in Table 6. The minimum titer of commercial antiserum must meet or exceed that of the BOB reference serum before release. The reactivity of the

---

The information in this chapter was adapted for the authors' use, with written permission, from DADE Division American Hospital Supply Corporation, P.O. Box 520672, Miami, Florida 33152 (17).

Table 6. Antisera minimum requirements[a]

Antisera	Test cell	Potency	Avidity
Anti-A	A_1	256	15 sec
	A_1B	128	30
	A_2	128	30
	A_2B	64	45
Anti-B	B	256	15
Anti-Rh$_o$ (D)	Rh$_o$ (D) positive	32	60

[a]As established by the Bureau of Biologics, Department of Health, Education, and Welfare.

reagents needs to be retested by the user for specificity, potency, and avidity. This must be done each time the reagents are received, even though they may be of the same lot number as the previous lot and are delivered to the same blood bank monthly.

Expiration Dates All antisera have an expiration date. Most liquid antisera have an expiration date of one year. Dried antisera last a bit longer. The blood bank must set up a system whereby the expiration date is called to the attention of the laboratory well in advance of the actual date. Obviously, expired antisera cannot be used. Dating must be checked upon receipt of the product.

Storage Conditions Manufacturers recommend storage at 2–8°C. Freezing is not recommended because it may lead to protein denaturation or the formation of precipitate-like residues.

Test Cells

Age Cells drawn on the day of testing usually will give better results than older cells.

Reactivity Good quality control dictates that the cell suspensions used be accurately prepared in the proper suspending medium. A negative control is essential to determine specificity of the reagent.

Titration Procedures

Two titration procedures are outlined below. Refer to Table 7 in following the steps.

Titration Procedure for ABO Blood Grouping Sera

1. Test cells: A_1, A_2, A_1B, B, A_2B, B.
2. Prepare a fresh 2% suspension of the specific cell to be tested in saline.

Table 7. Titer and avidity of test cells

	Titer		Avidity	
Cells	Concentration	Medium	Concentration	Medium
A & B	2%	Saline	10%	Saline
Rh_o (D)	2%	15% Albumin	40–50%	Whole blood (anticoagulated)

3. Set up a series of tubes, labeling them with the number of the dilution, e.g., 1, 2, 4, 8, 16, etc.
4. Beginning with the second tube and to each succeeding tube in the series, add 0.1 ml of saline.
5. Add 0.1 ml of the antiserum to be titered to tubes 1 and 2.
6. Mix tube 2 and deliver 0.1 ml of this mixture to tube 3. *Discard the pipette.*
7. With a clean pipette, mix contents of tube 3 and deliver 0.1 ml of the mixture to tube 4. *Discard the pipette.*
8. Carry out this doubling procedure to the expected endpoint of the serum titer.
9. Add 0.1 ml of the 2% cells from Step 2 to each tube.
10. Shake to mix and centrifuge for one minute at 1,000 RPM (RCF 125 g) or for 15–20 sec at 3,400 RPM (RCF 1,000 g). (RCF = Relative Centrifugal Force.)
11. Resuspend the cells and examine macroscopically for agglutination.

Titration Procedure for Rh-Hr Typing Sera

1. Test cells: Rh_o, $Rh_o{}'$, $Rh_o{}''$, $Rh_o{}'''$, hr′, hr‴, rh.
2. Prepare a fresh 2% suspension of the specific cell to be tested in 15% albumin.
3. Set up a series of test tube dilutions, e.g., 1, 2, 4, 8, 16, etc.
4. Beginning with the second tube and to each succeeding tube add 0.1 ml of 20% albumin.
5. Add 0.1 ml of antiserum to be titered to tubes 1 and 2.
6. Mix tube 2 and deliver 0.1 ml of this mixture to tube 3. *Discard the pipette.*
7. With a clean pipette, mix contents of tube 3 and deliver 0.1 ml of the mixture to tube 4. *Discard the pipette.*
8. Carry out this doubling dilution procedure to the expected endpoint of the serum titer.
9. Add 0.1 ml of 2% cells from Step 2 to each tube.

10. Shake to mix and incubate at 37°C for one hour.
11. Centrifuge as in Step 10 under Titration Procedure for ABO Blood Grouping Sera.
12. Resuspend the cells and examine macroscopically for agglutination.

Anti Human Globulin Serum

Frequency of Testing Testing should be done each day of use and whenever a new lot is received.

Determining the Ability of the Serum to React Quality Control test procedures enlist the use of antibodies such as Anti-Fy^a and Anti-Le^a to determine the ability of the antiglobulin serum to detect antibodies of different immunoglobulin classifications. These classes include IgG, IgA, IgM, and anticomplement.

Antigen Stability

(Reactivity of reagent red blood cell)

Frequency of Testing Testing should be done each day of use and whenever a new lot is received.

Method The procedure for testing antigen stability is as follows:

1. The reactivity of reagent red blood cells must be checked against positive and negative controls. The negative control can be obtained from any patient or donor whose serum does not contain antibody. The positive control will vary with the cell being tested.
2. To test reverse grouping, dilutions of Anti-A and Anti-B typing serums may be used. The test results should be 1–2+ before volume dilutions are made.
3. To test the antigen stability of cells employed in antibody screening and identification, the laboratory probably will need to purchase commercial sera. Those antigens whose stability should be routinely tested are D, M, N, P, Le^a, and Fy^a. The reaction sought here is 1–2+.
4. Reagent cells also should be checked for hemolysis before they are used. It is the authors' opinion that cells showing even a small amount of hemolysis should not be used because hemolysis indicates deterioration of the red blood cell.
5. Bovine albumin: Testing should be done each day of use and whenever a new lot arrives. Macroscopic and microscopic observation of the solution will ensure the absence of hemolysis, crenation, or rouleaux formation. The use of a positive control, Anti-Rh$_o$ (D) should give no reaction in saline, but a positive reaction should occur when albumin is added. The use of a negative control is required to assure the user of specificity.

6. Physiological saline: If this reagent is prepared in-house, prepare the saline (0.85% w/v) in large amounts, aliquot in quantities sufficient to last one working day, and sterilize either by filtration or in an autoclave. The storage container should be of borosilicate glass that has been washed in dilute nitric acid (1:1), rinsed in tap water, and given a final rinse in distilled water 15 times. Sterile physiological saline also is available commercially.

All of the above procedure for antigen stability must be documented and properly recorded.

INSTRUMENT CONTROL

Centrifuges

The packing of the cell button during centrifugation is directly proportional to the speed and time of centrifugation. It is necessary to calibrate the centrifuge over its normal working range, i.e., for each type of test performed on it.

Calibration of Fixed-Speed Centrifuges For high protein tube calibration, select an antibody that gives a 2+ reaction by your current techniques for high protein testing. Anti-Rh_0 (D) typing serum may be used, and a 2+ reaction can be selected by using a titration and doubling serial dilutions. Pick cell types that will give both a positive and negative reaction for the antibody involved.

Saline and Enzyme Calibrations Select an antibody that gives a 2+ reaction by your current technique. Set up the serum-cell mixtures only when ready to centrifuge so that any inconsistencies caused by cells settling in the serum will not be introduced. When the proper setting for centrifugation is found, the supernatant fluid will be clear and the cell button well defined. The final time selected must show the strongest reaction with the positive cell and a clear-cut negative reaction with the negative cell. When the final selection is made, it should be marked on the centrifuge so that all personnel are aware of the proper setting.

Calibration Control of Variable Speed Centrifuges

When several different speeds are attainable with a centrifuge, the laboratory must determine the RCF (Relative Centrifugal Force) required for each specific test by referring to the manufacturer's package instructions. Once the RCF is known, a simple calculation turns RCF into RPM. By using the formula $RCF = 1.118 \times 10^{-5} n^2 r$ (when n is speed in RPM,

Quality Control Reference Red Blood Cells

Lot # _____ Received _____ Expiration Date _____

Date	Anti-A Lot # _____				Anti-B Lot # _____				Anti-A,B Lot # _____				Anti-Rh (D) Lot #____		AHG Lot #	Saline Lot # _____				BB Tech.
	Q.C. Cells				Q.C. Cells				Q.C. Cells				Q.C. Cells			Q.C. Cells				
	A_1	A_2	B	O+	A_1	A_2	B	O+	A_1	A_2	B	O+	O+	O-	CPC	A_1	A_2	B	CPC	
	Tube #				Tube #				Tube #				Tube #			Tube #				
	7A	8A	9A	10A	7B	8B	9B	10B	7AB	8AB	9AB	10AB	10D	11D	12C	7S	8S	9S	12S	

DADE DIVISION AMERICAN HOSPITAL SUPPLY CORPORATION P.O. BOX 520672 MIAMI • FLORIDA x 33152

BB563-H

Figures 3a–3g. Blood banking record-keeping forms. (Reproduced with permission from DADE Division American Hospital Supply Corporation, P.O. Box 520672, Miami, Florida 33152.) Figure 3a. Daily identity record: Quality control reference red blood cells.

Quality Control Reference Serums

Lot # _____ Received _____ Expiration Date _____

daily identity record

Date	A_1 Cells Lot # _____				B. Cells Lot # _____				O Rh_o (D) Pos. Cells Lot # _____					O-Neg Cells # ___	Coombs Control Cells Lot # _____			BB Tech.
	Anti-A	Anti-B	Anti-A,B,	Saline	Anti-A	Anti-B	Anti-A,B	Saline	Anti-A	Anti-B	Anti-A,B	Anti-D	Saline	Anti-D	Anti-Human Serum	Saline		
	Tube #				Tube #				Tube #						Tube #			
	1A	2A	3A	6A	1B	2B	3B	6B	1O	2O	3O	4O	6O	4O	5C	6C		

© 1973 DADE DIVISION A.H.S.C.

Figure 3b. Daily identity record: Quality control reference serums.

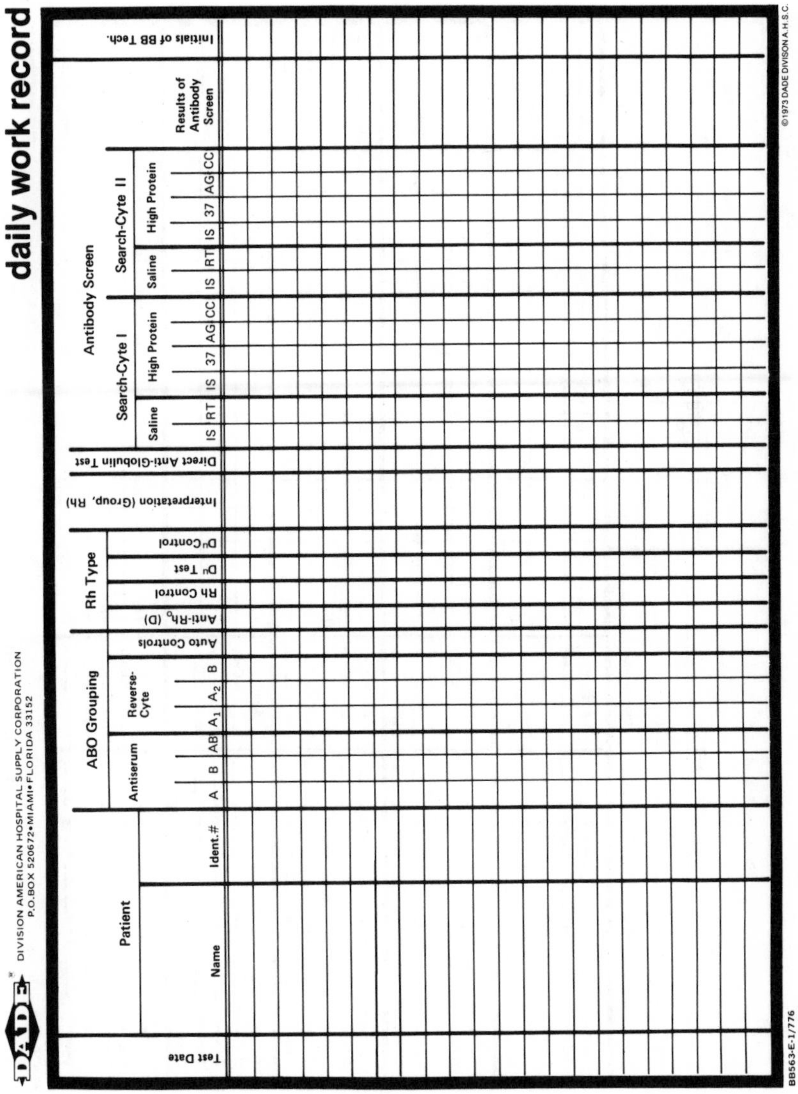

Figure 3c. Daily work record.

Figure 3d. Antiserum specificity, titer, and avidity record.

Figure 3e. Compatibility test record.

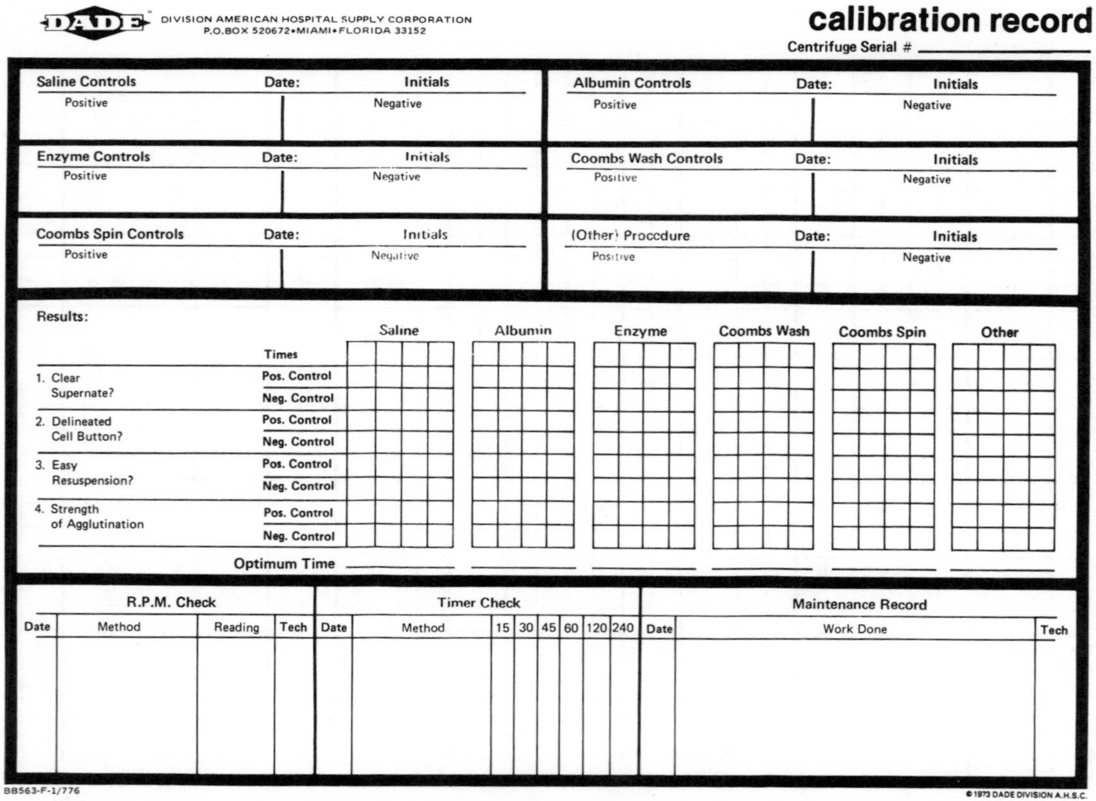

DADE™ DIVISION AMERICAN HOSPITAL SUPPLY CORPORATION
P.O.BOX 520672•MIAMI•FLORIDA 33152

calibration record

Centrifuge Serial # ____________

Saline Controls	Date:	Initials	Albumin Controls	Date:	Initials
Positive		Negative	Positive		Negative

Enzyme Controls	Date:	Initials	Coombs Wash Controls	Date:	Initials
Positive		Negative	Positive		Negative

Coombs Spin Controls	Date:	Initials	(Other) Procedure	Date:	Initials
Positive		Negative	Positive		Negative

Results:

	Times	Saline	Albumin	Enzyme	Coombs Wash	Coombs Spin	Other
1. Clear Supernate?	Pos. Control						
	Neg. Control						
2. Delineated Cell Button?	Pos. Control						
	Neg. Control						
3. Easy Resuspension?	Pos. Control						
	Neg. Control						
4. Strength of Agglutination	Pos. Control						
	Neg. Control						
	Optimum Time						

R.P.M. Check

Date	Method	Reading	Tech

Timer Check

Date	Method	15	30	45	60	120	240

Maintenance Record

Date	Work Done	Tech

BB563-F-1/776

Figure 3f. Calibration record.

DADE® DIVISION AMERICAN HOSPITAL SUPPLY CORPORATION
P.O.BOX 520672•MIAMI•FLORIDA 33152

instrument temperature record

Date	Time	Heat Bath				View Box				Refrigerator or Freezer				BB Tech.
		I.D.#	I.D.#	I.D.#	I.D.#	I.D.#	I.D.#	I.D.#	I.D.#	I.D.#	I.D.#	I.D.#	I.D.#	

Date	Time	Heat Bath				View Box				Refrigerator or Freezer				BB Tech.
		I.D.#	I.D.#	I.D.#	I.D.#	I.D.#	I.D.#	I.D.#	I.D.#	I.D.#	I.D.#	I.D.#	I.D.#	

BB563-I-1/776

Figure 3g. Instrument temperature record.

and r is the head radius in centimeters measured from the motor shaft center line to the extreme of the tube in its rotating position), RPM can be calculated (18). This step must be performed before following the steps listed under Calibration of Fixed-Speed Centrifuges.

DATA HANDLING AND RECORDING

The objective of data recording is to provide a uniform system of control and documentation of test and quality control results. Since different licensing and accrediting agencies have different requirements for record-keeping, it is the responsibility of the laboratory to contact their agency for detailed information. The prime consideration for record-keeping is daily consistency and clarity.

The record-keeping forms, reproduced as Figures 3a–3g, were developed by DADE Diagnostic (18) and are used in the authors' laboratory. For In-Process Control (Technique), the reader is urged to follow the American Association of Blood Banking recommendations (19). The reader also may wish to further supplement this material with reference 20.

chapter seven

Quality Control in Clinical Chemistry

REAGENTS, SOLVENTS, AND CHEMICALS

Card File System

The chemistry laboratory should maintain a card file system listing all reagents, solvents, and chemicals used in the analyses. Each card should show the grade of the reagent, the company from which it was purchased, the purity as specified by the company and required by the technique, and expiration dates, if any. Upon receipt of a reagent, solvent, or chemical, the date received and date opened should be recorded on the container. Before use, reagent acceptability should be ascertained by running the reagent as a blank in the procedure for which it was designed.

Reagent Grade

For most clinical chemistry procedures, Analytical Reagent Grade is satisfactory. More sensitive techniques such as atomic absorption, spectroscopy, or gas chromatography may require purer solvents, such as spectroquality or chromatoquality solvents.

Freshly Prepared Reagents

Freshly prepared reagents should be tested in parallel with reagents already in use to ensure that the new reagent is suitable for use. Reference materials and calibrators must be within acceptable limits with the new reagents.

Reagent Blank

Analysts must determine the background response of each of the reagents and solvents used in the analytical procedure under the same conditions used for unknowns. If significant amounts of interfering substances are present, new and satisfactory reagents and solvents must be obtained for

43

the analysis. An interfering substance may be significant in only one procedure, or it may affect the results of several determinations, depending on the substance and procedure.

PRIMARY STANDARDS

Primary standards are substances of known stability and known activity. The physical properties and reactivity of the primary standard are completely known and when possible are certified by an authority such as the National Bureau of Standards (NBS). These substances are always in pure form (>99%).

Obtaining Primary Standards

Primary standards must be obtained from a reliable source, accurately prepared in calibrated volumetric glassware, and stored in containers that will not alter the reagent. Several primary standards are available from the NBS for substances that are important in the clinical laboratory. Secondary (certified) standards also may be obtained from many chemical companies, along with a statement of their purity.

Use of Primary Standards

Primary standards may be used to maintain quality control as follows:

1. To calibrate instruments. As an example, the didymium filter for a Coleman Jr. Spectrophotometer is considered a primary standard. However, this filter is subject to decay with time, approximately 1% per year. Therefore, use didymium filters for wavelength calibration only, not as photometric standards. Photometric standards may be purchased for linearity checks. Certified (NBS) chemicals are considered primary standards. All instruments should be calibrated as specified by the Clinical Laboratory Improvement Act (CLIA) or the College of American Pathologists (CAP) using a primary standard.
2. To ensure the accuracy of a procedure.
3. To determine the acceptability of in-house standards, i.e., secondary standards used in the day-to-day analysis. Remember that a primary standard is pure and must be treated properly to maintain its purity and usefulness. Do not remove the material from its container with a spatula: Pour the material into a beaker; replace the cap immediately. Weigh from the beaker and discard the residual amount. Do not return it to the stock bottle.

CONTROLS OR REFERENCE MATERIALS

Controls are stable under storage conditions, the physical properties are similar to actual specimens, and the entire pool is (or should be) homogeneous. While primary and secondary standards are used to check the sensitivity of the instrument and procedure, the control is used to detect variability in the analytical procedure. The control is carried through the same preparative and analytical procedures that are followed for unknown samples. Both normal and abnormal controls should be analyzed with each group of specimens. If the control falls within the predetermined limits of precision and accuracy (refer to Chapter 5, Statistical Quality Control, of this manual), the analyst has some assurance that the analytical procedure is in control and that results on the unknowns are reliable. Recall that using two standard deviations as control limits, 5% of the time (one out of 20 specimens) a reference value may be outside ±2S and the procedure is still in statistical control. (See Chapter 5.)

Preparation or Purchase of Controls?

The question of whether one should prepare or purchase controls is in part dependent on the financial resources and the capabilities of the laboratory. The preparation of a control pool is lengthy and laborious. Most clinical laboratories are well advised to purchase control material. The difference between assayed and unassayed material is that assayed material has been analyzed enough to establish an accepted value and is therefore more expensive. If the method used to assay the material is not the same one that the purchasing laboratory will use, assayed value is of little use, and the material must be assayed in laboratory; if the same method is used, material still must be checked in laboratory because the material's level of performance may be quite different from that recorded by the commercial or contract laboratory which initially assayed the material.

Assayed Controls Assayed controls are usually commercially prepared serum pools to which known amounts of biological constituents such as bilirubin, amylase, etc., have been added. Before releasing the product for sale, the manufacturer has the control analyzed by several independent laboratories. Mean and standard deviations are determined for each test, and a package insert with all the necessary information accompanies the serum to your laboratory. For example, this laboratory uses one manufacturer's assayed normal and abnormal sera with over forty biological constituents. The assayed control may be used to measure accuracy and precision under actual conditions. Note that a normal assayed pool and an abnormal assayed pool must be run concurrent with the test specimens.

Unassayed Controls   Several manufacturers market normal and abnormal unassayed lyophilized control material. Unassayed pools are less costly than assayed pools, but keep in mind that, with an unassayed serum, accuracy under actual conditions is unknown for some time. Because of a lack of funds, many laboratories prepare a frozen pool serum which they have gathered from fasting, normal patients' sera and fasting blood donors.

Our laboratory prepares normal and abnormal control sera as follows: Collect only clear serum samples free of hemolysis, lipemia, icterus, or dyes. Freeze at $0°C$. Repeat daily until a quantity sufficient to last one year has been accumulated. Serum must be analyzed each day before freezing to ensure that it is normal serum; otherwise, you may ruin the entire pool. Once the desired volume has been attained, proceed with the following:

1. Normal pool:

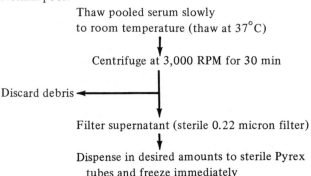

          Thaw pooled serum slowly
          to room temperature (thaw at $37°C$)

          Centrifuge at 3,000 RPM for 30 min

Discard debris ◄───

          Filter supernatant (sterile 0.22 micron filter)

          Dispense in desired amounts to sterile Pyrex
          tubes and freeze immediately

2. Abnormal pool: Before dispensing, add desired constituents (such as glucose, bilirubin, bicarbonate, or amylase) in the amount necessary to produce desired levels (usually critical diagnostic levels), and mix thoroughly. For example, bilirubin values of 1.0–20 mg, glucose at 100–70 mg, or creatinine at 0.5–1.3 mg. Analyze the pool to make certain that the desired levels have been reached. (Refer to page 28.)

Be aware of changes in variability as shown by controls as they appear on the Shewhart Charts. A trend on a Shewhart Quality Control Chart occurs when five or more consecutive control values (means) increase or decrease. A shift may be identified when, over a three-day period, five or six consecutive values fall on the same side of the central line. Excessive variability may be identified by points falling outside the control limits. Causes of control chart problems are discussed on pages 26–28.

INSTRUMENTATION (GENERAL)

Instruments

Instruments used in clinical chemistry include the analytical balance, the pH meter, the conductivity meter, the spectrophotometer, temperature devices, selective ion electrodes, and the atomic absorption spectrophotometer.

Analytical Balance If the balance is not accurate to ±0.01 mg, all data related to weight-prepared standards will reflect the same degree of error. To ensure accurate weights, adhere to the following criteria. (Note: Do not handle weights with hands.)

1. The balance should be mounted on a heavy table away from extreme heat or cold and vibration.
2. The level of the balance should be checked daily and adjusted when necessary.
3. When not in use, all weight should be taken off the balance, and the balance should be placed in the full arrest position and covered.
4. The balance accuracy should be checked weekly, using certified class S-1 weights ranging from 10.0 mg to 100.0 g. Results should be recorded.

pH Meter Before use, the instrument should be standardized with buffers of pH 4.0, 7.0, and 10.0 which may be purchased from a reliable source. The results should be recorded. Before testing the pH of a sample, the meter must be checked with pH in the range of the test solution.

Electrodes The level of saturated KCl in the calomel electrode should be checked weekly; replace KCl when necessary. When not in use, the electrode should be immersed in distilled water. Glass electrodes have slow response time in highly buffered solutions, and, for this reason, all samples requiring a pH check must be stirred during measurement.

Conductivity Meter The ability of water to conduct an electric current is directly proportional to the dissolved metallic ions in the water. Conductance is an excellent general indicator of the quality of water, but keep in mind that dissolved gases, which also act as electrolytes, are not measured with this instrument.

For the most accurate use of the conductivity meter, the following procedure should be performed (see Table 8):

1. Standardize the cell by measuring the conductivity of a standard KCl solution.

Table 8. Electrical conductivity of KCl solutions

Normality	Preparation	Temperature ($^\circ$C)	Conductivity (μmhos)
0.1	7.4365 g KCl/liter	25°C	12,856
0.01	0.7440 g KCl/liter	25°C	1,408

For instruments reading in mhos, calculate the cell constant as follows:

$$L = \frac{K_1 + K_2}{1{,}000{,}000 \times K_x}$$

where, L = cell constant
K_1 = μmhos of KCl solution
K_2 = μmhos of distilled water used to prepare the solution
K_x = mhos

2. Ranges: lead 0.5–15.0 μg/ml; copper 0.15–5.0 μg/ml.
3. Immerse the cell in the sample several times before obtaining a reading.

Selective Ion Electrodes Selective ion electrodes measure specific ion activity. The electrodes do not measure concentrations of non-ionized material. The fluoride and chloride electrodes are used as a means of reducing analytical work and improving the quality of the data. When the electrode malfunctions, the same checks used for the pH meter should be applied.

Atomic Absorption Spectrophotometer
Calibration Procedure for Blood Lead Analysis:

1. Using certified primary standards, prepare a fresh 100 μg/ml stock solution. Prepare working standards over the range of concentrations that may be encountered in an analysis.
2. Ranges: lead 0.5–15.0 μg/ml; copper 0.15–5.0 μg/ml.
3. The standard solutions should be used one time only. The stock solution is to be discarded also.
4. Make the necessary adjustments for start up (refer to instruction manual), analyze the series of standards, and record the absorbance values.
5. Prepare a calibration curve on linear graph paper, plotting absorbance values against the concentration of each standard in μg/ml. Prepare another curve by plotting readings obtained on the concentration mode (as ppm).
6. The similarity of the two curves will attest to the precision or reproducibility but not to the accuracy of the instrument.

Instrument Identification No. _____

Mandatory Calibration Interval _____

Date Last Calibration _____

Date Next Calibration _____

Primary Metal Used for Calibration _____

Chemist's Signature _____

Figure 4. Sample calibration control card to be attached to each atomic absorption spectrophotometer.

Documentation: The curves generated by using the certified primary standards are to be labeled and kept on file. On each instrument, in plain view, there should be a calibration control card bearing the information shown on the sample card in Figure 4.

Frequency: Calibration should be performed at weekly intervals and whenever new lots of reagents, standards, and controls are introduced. All curves and control cards should be filed for at least two years.

SUPPORTIVE SERVICES

Water

Distilled, demineralized, glass-redistilled water should be used for the preparation of reagents and standards.

Analysis The pH and conductivity of the water should be measured weekly and recorded. Further checks on a monthly basis include hardness and concentration of zinc, iron, manganese, potassium, sodium, calcium, magnesium, silica, and amines. Water quality is acceptable when the concentration of each metal does not exceed 0.01 ppm, test of hardness is *negative*, silica is negative, and amines are negative. The pH should not be less than 5.5 and conductance should be 10.0 μmhos or less. Distilled demineralized water is acceptable for other laboratory uses.

Ammonia-free Water If the laboratory needs ammonia-free water in limited volumes, "Quikpure" (Box 254, Chicago, Illinois), 500-ml bottles, may be used, but, for larger volumes, immediate collection of distilled water which has been passed through a mixed bed demineralizer is recommended.

CO_2-free Water Immediate collection from the second glass distillation is required. The carboy for storage should be fitted with a glass drying tube containing CaO_2 or $CaCl_2$ indicator.

Electrical Services

Voltage Regulation Spectrophotometers, flame photometers, atomic absorption equipment, auto-analyzers, and gas chromatographs have complicated circuitry that requires current with constant voltage to maintain sensitivity and stable, drift-free operation. To eliminate voltage fluctuation, in-line voltage regulators may be factory-installed or added subsequently. If your equipment suddenly experiences baseline drift or erratic behavior, be sure the voltage regulator is operational. Further action may be necessary. Consult the instrument manual for recommendations.

Bottled Oxidant and Fuels

Bottled gases should be purchased from a reliable source. Each tank should be checked for purity before use by observing baselines on standby.

Glassware

Storage Types Borosilicate or Nalgene containers should be used for storage of reagents and standards. Strong alkalies or solvents must be stored in borosilicate glass, not Nalgene. Silica, boron, and the alkali metals, however, must be stored in Nalgene containers because borosilicate glass is not completely inert to them.

Washing Procedures The steps in ordinary and special washing procedures are listed below.

Ordinary	Special
1. Tap water and detergent	1. 1:1 nitric acid (rinse)
2. Tap water rinse	2. Tap water rinse
3. Final distilled water rinse	3. Distilled water rinse 15 times
4. Dry	4. Dry

DAILY QUESTIONNAIRE

The questionnaires, reproduced as Figures 5a and 5b, were designed by Dr. David Boyze of the Center for Disease Control as an aid to quality

Figure 5a. Daily questionnaire designed as an aid to quality control in the clinical chemistry laboratory. (Designed by Dr. David Boyze of the Center for Disease Control, and reproduced with permission.)

QUALITY CONTROL PROGRAM
Daily Questionnaire

Date _____ Time _____

Analysis _____ Technician _____

Daily Section

1. Any new standards? . . . . .Yes__No__

2. Any new reagents? . . . . .Yes__No__

3. Are any controls in Range 2? .Yes__No__

4. Have you done daily stability checks on both IL flame
   photometers? . . . . .Yes__No__

   Set with 140/5 standards. Aspirate lithium and reread the
   standard dilution used for original settings. Na should
   not vary + 1.0 Meq/liter. K should not vary + 0.1 Meq/liter.
   Lithium level should remain between indicator lines. Are
   both instruments stable? . . . . .Yes__No__

5. Did you drain water traps at air gauge and on compressor
   tank? . . . . .Yes__No__

6. Are the Beckman B, Coleman Jr., and Klett in proper
   working order? . . . . .Yes__No__

7. Have any of the previous results been questioned? . . . . . .Yes__No__

Friday Section

8. Are there sufficient reagents for the weekend? . . . . .Yes__No__

9. Is there a sufficient quantity of cups and gas for the
   flame photometer? . . . . .Yes__No__

10. Has a linearity check on the flame photometers
    been done? . . . . .Yes__No__

	100/2	140/5	160/8
No. 1		Set	
No. 2		Set	

11. Has the atomizer been cleaned this week? . . . . .Yes__No__

12. Have the chimney and burner been cleaned within
    two weeks? . . . . .Yes__No__

Other Problems? _____

QUALITY CONTROL PROGRAM
Daily Questionnaire

Date_____ Technician_____

Turntable

1. Have you cleaned up all spillage on and around turntable? .Yes__No__

2. Is the turntable missing samples or picking up twice? . . . . .Yes__No__

3. Has the reservoir been cleaned? . . . . .Yes__No__

Pump

1. Have the pumps been oiled today? (monthly). . . . . .Yes__No__

2. Have the rollers been cleaned with methanol
today? (weekly). . . . . .Yes__No__

Heating Baths And Dialyzers

1. Are all heating baths at the proper temperature? . . . . .Yes__No__

2. Which heating bath needed adjustment? . . . . ._____

3. Are all dialyzers free of plugs? . . . . .Yes__No__

4. Which dialyzers were changed today?
Glu __ BUN __ KNa __ Cl __CO$_2$ __

Colorimeters

1. Are all colorimeters balanced and at proper energy?. . . . . .Yes__No__

2. Have the optics and filters been cleaned today? (monthly) .Yes__No__

3. Is the tubing to and from flowcell free of deposits? . . . . . .Yes__No__

Flame

1. Did you blow out the capillary today? . . . . .Yes__No__

2. Did you clean the fan filter today? (weekly). . . . . .Yes__No__

3. Has the chimney been cleaned today?. . . . . .Yes__No__

4. Have the filters been cleaned today? (weekly). . . . . .Yes__No__

Figure 5b. Daily questionnaire designed as an aid to quality control in the clinical chemistry laboratory. (Designed by Dr. David Boyze of the Center for Disease Control, and reproduced with permission.)

Recorder

1. Do you have an ample reserve of chart paper?
   (Special order). . . . . .Yes__No__

2. Is the recorder in need of repair?. . . . . .Yes__No__

General Maintenance

1. Do you have an ample supply of gas?. . . . . .Yes__No__

2. Has the compressor been drained today?. . . . . .Yes__No__

3. Was all spillage cleaned out of reagent trays? . . . . .Yes__No__

4. Does the instrument need retubing?. . . . . .Yes__No__

5. Tubing replaced . . . All _____ Part_____

   _____

6. Which channels were rephased today?_____

7. Did you expand the Na and Cl scales? . . . . .Yes__No__

8. Were any of your controls in Range 2?. . . . . .Yes__No__

9. Have any of your results been questioned? . . . . .Yes__No__

10. No. of I.Q.__L.A.__Reason _____

11. Standards used_____ Time diluted _____

12. Any new reagents? (Circle)

    Wash valve H_2O . . . BUN color . . . BUN Acid . . .

    BUN H_2O. . . CO_2 color . . . H_2SO_4 . . . Chloride Color . . . . .

    Nitric Acid . . . Chloride H_2O. . . Glucose Color . . .

    NaCl . . . Sodium Carbonate . . . Lithium . . . KNa H_2O. . .

    Hi-Lo Stds . . . .

Other Problems_____

_____

_____

assurance in the clinical chemistry laboratory. They also can be used to obtain feedback information. Use these to check your laboratory's efficiency.

DAY-BY-DAY QUALITY CONTROL

The following outline represents the day-by-day quality control practiced in the Clinical Chemistry Section of the authors' laboratory. This outline was obtained from the Clinical Laboratory Improvement Act: Guidelines for Quality Control, 1967.

1. Specimen Condition:
   From all sources. To be described in detail in the procedures manual developed in the laboratory.
2. Precision of Methods (before a procedure is used):
   a. By determining normal ranges and sensitivity to abnormal ranges.
   b. By use of reference methods and reference materials.
   c. All records or references concerning the validity of a procedure and the percentage of laboratories using the procedure are maintained in the laboratory for as long as that procedure is used.
3. Automated Testing Requirements:
   a. Calibration:
      1) Daily—using the required number of standards and blanks described in the American Monitor Corporation Application Notes for each analyte before specimen analysis and with each group of 35–40 samples.
      2) Whenever—new lots of standards, controls, and reagents are introduced.
      3) Manual Calibration—using one blank and at least four different concentrations of standards that span the significant analytical range. This must be done before analyzing unknown samples.
   b. Calibration Records:
      1) Automated—Record the range on the Shewhart Charts prepared in-house. The *factor** must be recorded on the plots and in the record book as well. Acceptable deviation limits for the factor and the standard must be established for each new lot. (*Factor refers to a value calculated by the Programmachem Unit used in the authors' laboratory to analyze serum for chemical constituents.)
      2) Manual—With each run, draw a calibration curve using the

blank as zero and the four values of the standards for each analysis. Post as with all other records.

3) New Lots or Batches of Lots—Before use, a new reagent, standard, or control must be tested to ensure that it meets performance criteria. (Refer to the section on reagents and chemicals at the beginning of this chapter.) With each new lot of standards, controls, and reagents, the instrument must be recalibrated using the Standards furnished by the American Monitor Corporation, and the results must be properly recorded. (Note: When available, the calibrators used are to be certified by NBS. A document can be obtained from American Monitor tracing the lineage of the 2,000 level standards to NBS. This document should be available on file in the laboratory.)

4) Acceptable Deviation Limits—are to be defined for all calibrators as previously described.

c. Controls:
Normal and abnormal assayed serum controls are purchased from Lederle Diagnostics. These controls are to be used before analysis and randomly distributed between every 10th specimen.

d. Recording Control Results:
Lederle's assayed control furnishes the mean, standard deviation (upper control limit, lower control limit), and coefficient of variation on each lot of assayed sera.

e. Daily Recording:
All out-of-control results require remedial action (refer to procedures manual and documentation). Control charts must include, as a minimum, $\overline{X} \pm 2S$, lot number of the reference material, and date of analysis. These charts should be posted in the laboratory, and results should be recorded as they are developed.

f. Precision:
After the 10th specimen, a repeat analysis of the first patient's specimen is made. The ranges of the replicates are kept until 30 specimens have been determined. An estimate of the standard deviation is calculated from these data and posted on separate Shewhart Charts. (For method of determining precision, refer to p. 22).

g. Precision Limits:
These should not exceed $\overline{X} \pm 2S$ established in-house based on the previous month's work nor exceed a coefficient of variation (CV)

of 5%. Na and Cl should have a CV $\leqslant$2%. Enzyme determinations should not exceed a CV of 10%.

h. Testing Upon Arrival:

Each new lot, shipment, or preparation of calibrators and controls should be tested concurrently with the previous batch in use before being placed into routine use. The results should be recorded appropriately along with those of the previous lot before the new lot is used. This need only be performed one time, upon arrival.

4. Reagent Control:

Before use, each new lot of reagent is tested for interfering materials by comparison with the previous lot of reagent and by running the controls and standards with the new reagent. Information on the date received, date opened, and expiration date should be recorded both on the container and in the appropriate record form. Storage conditions should be described on the reagent control card.

5. Temperature Control:

Daily, the temperature of the water bath in the Programmachem Unit is checked. The results are to be recorded. The thermometer is to be labeled (date calibrated, temperature, error noted) after calibration at monthly intervals with a NBS Thermometer.

6. Volumetric Glassware:

All volumetric glassware (autodiluters, pipettes, volumetric flasks, graduate cylinders, etc.) is to be checked periodically for accuracy. Both the gravimetric procedure and the volumetric procedure are acceptable. In this laboratory, the volumetric procedure will generally be used as follows:

a. Dispense measured volumes of distilled water at 25°C from the glassware being checked into a certified TC Volumetric Flask until the flask is filled.

b. Compare the volume dispensed with the location of the meniscus in the flask.

c. The NBS tolerances are listed in Table 9.

7. Storage Type of Glassware:

a. Borosilicate or Nalgene containers are to be used for storage of reagents and standards. Strong alkalies are not to be stored in borosilicate glass because borosilicate glass is not completely inert to alkalies. These solutions must be stored in Nalgene containers.

b. Cleaning of Glassware (routine).

1) Wash in Alconox.

2) Thoroughly rinse in tap water.

Table 9. Allowable limits of error (volumetric glassware)

Capacity (ml)	Type	Allowable limits of error (ml)
	Pipettes: autodilutors	
2.0		0.006
5.0		0.01
10.0		0.02
25.0		0.025
	Graduated flasks (cylinders)	
25.0		0.03
50.0		0.05
100.0		0.08
500.0		0.15
1,000.0		0.50

For anything with a capacity less than 1 ml, the gravimetric procedure must be used to determine allowable limits of error.

    3) Make a final rinse in distilled and/or demineralized water (15–20 times).

8. Demineralized Water:

In order to be acceptable for clinical laboratory use, the distilled and/or demineralized water must meet the following specifications: 1) pH 5.5–7.0, 2) conductivity 10 μmhos or less, 3) metals $\leqslant$0.01 ppm or less, 4) orthophosphates–negative, and 5) bacteria–negative. pH and conductivity must be determined weekly and records kept on the appropriate form. Metals, phosphates, and bacterial suitability must be tested quarterly.

9. Preventive Maintenance:

Refer to p. 9.

chapter eight Quality Control in Hematology

HEMATOLOGY QUALITY CONTROL

As with all other areas in the clinical laboratory, a well designed quality control program will eliminate the necessity of managing hematology procedures by crisis.

Many texts on quality control in hematology devote the majority of the discussion to the beneficial aspect of having a program. Recognizing that most laboratorians reading this text will be past the point of wondering whether or not to have a program, the remainder of this chapter is an abbreviated outline of a quality control system that should ensure the quality of data generated and satisfy laboratory licensure requirements.

Validation of Methods Used in Hematology

Before instituting a new procedure in the laboratory, the sensitivity of the procedure must be determined and the procedure must be validated by the use of certified standards and controls. Documentation of the references for the procedure, as well as a written description of the method or methods used to validate the procedure, must be kept on file in the laboratory for as long as the procedure is used. The documents should include a statement by the supervisor and director to the effect that the procedure has been found to meet all requirements (internal and external) and has their written approval for use in the laboratory. This must be done with every procedure employed in the clinical laboratory. (Refer to Day-by-day Quality Control, p. 54.)

Specific Quality Control Measures

Standards Where a certified standard exists, such as certified cyanmethemoglobin standard, the laboratory is obliged to calibrate all instruments with this standard in the following manner:

1. Once a month, or whenever new lots of reagents, controls, or standards are received, the linearity of the procedure must be verified by per-

forming the procedure with no less than three (preferably four) concentrations of the standard.

2. The results of the calibration must be plotted on a graph and a standard curve determined by linear regression analysis, or the best visual fit of the line to the coordinates obtained, after performing the procedure with the standards. Since linear regression analysis is impractical for most laboratories, the best visual fit is acceptable.

3. The curve must be posted with the following information: 1) date of calibration, 2) standard used for calibration, including lot number and expiration date of the standard, 3) name of procedure used, 4) wavelength, control settings, etc., used to perform the calibration, and 5) initials of technician or technologist.

4. This curve is to be maintained in an active file for one month, or until the next calibration is performed. As with all other quality control records, the curves must be kept for two years.

5. The instrument should have the date of the last calibration posted in plain view to remind the analyst of the next calibration date. (Refer to Clinical Chemistry, p. 49, and Figure 4.)

With automated equipment, it is not unrealistic to expect the laboratory to perform a calibration as frequently as once a day, or at least to analyze two standards (high concentration and low concentration) at the beginning of each work day and with each change of shift. With manual procedures, the analyst must include at least two standards each time the test is performed.

Controls Several manufacturers distribute assayed hematology controls. The controls (normal and abnormal) must be included twice a day, results must fall between the pre-established limits specified by the manufacturer, and the control results should be posted in plain view on Shewhart Charts supplied by the company or prepared in-house. Assayed controls can serve as accuracy checks.

Precision At least one out of every ten patients' specimens should be analyzed in duplicate and the results of both tests recorded. Once the laboratory obtains 30 duplicates, the precision for the procedure can be determined. The method for determining precision is explained in detail on p. 22.

Coefficient of Variation (CV) A coefficient of variation of less than 5% is indicative of good precision. The reader is referred to p. 19 for determining coefficient of variation. To check the CV, repeat the analysis of *one specimen* 10 times, determine the mean of the 10 values, and calculate the CV.

Repeats of Abnormals If any result from a patient falls outside the predetermined "Normal Limits," the test must be repeated and the result recorded. In addition to this, Medicare regulations require that:

1. Specimens that have a WBC $> 50 \times 10^9$ ($50,000/cm^3$) must be repeated by dilution ($25,000/mm^3$ by manual methods).
2. Specimens that have a WBC $< 3.0 \times 10^9$ ($3,000/cm^3$) must be repeated.
3. Specimens that have a RBC $> 7.0 \times 10^{12}$ ($7,000,000/cm^3$) must be repeated by dilution.
4. Specimens that have a RBC $< 3.0 \times 10^{12}$ ($3,000,000/cm^3$) must be repeated.
5. Specimens that have a hemoglobin <10 g/dl must be rediluted and repeated.

Reagents Each new lot of reagents must be tested with normal and abnormal controls and with specimen replicates before they are used. If the accuracy and precision of the procedure are maintained, the reagent may be released for routine use. The results of such testing, along with the initials of the examiner and signature of the chief technologist, must be properly recorded.

Autodilutors The autodilutor must be checked for accuracy and reproducibility by the following method:

1. Accuracy (daily): Make sure that standards, controls, and replicates are within acceptable limits.
2. Reproducibility (quarterly): Allow the autodiluter to dispense into a certified TC Volumetric Flask. (Refer to p. 11.) Record as "acceptable" if the level of the meniscus does not exceed ±0.01 ml. Record the results of this determination on the appropriate record-keeping form.

Special Requirements The hematocrit test has special requirements which must be observed:

1. The centrifuge RPM must be checked quarterly (refer to Preventive Maintenance, p. 12).
2. Microhematocrit tests performed on capillary blood must be run in duplicate.
3. Normal and abnormal controls should be tested and the results documented with each batch of specimens performed.

Preventive Maintenance Refer to the section on Preventive Maintenance in Chapter 4, p. 9.

Differentials All slides must be labeled and saved for one month. As an added quality control measure, the laboratory director should repeat daily a certain percentage of the differentials performed by the technologists and technicians. These also must be recorded. It is essential that the hematology laboratory maintain a collection of abnormal differentials to serve as training aids and comparisons to questionable differentials. An atlas of hematology would seem to be a prerequisite for a good hematology laboratory. Using the differential as a comparison with the other parameters (WBC, RBC, HCT, HGB) has always been a good quality control check.

COAGULATION QUALITY ASSURANCE

General Considerations

To ensure coagulation quality, the following laboratory procedures are recommended:

1. The requisition slip must be designed to provide for submission of pertinent information on bleeding history, anticoagulant drugs, and other medication.
2. A daily log (worksheet) of results of all coagulation studies should be maintained. The analyst simply needs to record patient name, patient number, and results, along with control results.
3. All specimens must be analyzed as soon as received in the laboratory. Should this become impossible, a limit of two hours after receipt can be imposed, provided the specimens have been collected and stored properly.
4. Each specimen must be tested in duplicate, results recorded, and range determined. Once 30 determinations have been made, the results can be used to calculate precision limits. Shewhart Charts must be maintained from that point on. Refer to p. 22.
5. A control in the normal range and abnormal range must be included for each batch of specimens tested. Control results must be plotted on Shewhart Charts and recorded on the analysis request form.
6. Acceptable deviation limits must be specified for each control, and results must fall within the manufacturers' predetermined limits.
7. Control charts and records must include the mean, the upper, and the lower limits, the lot number of controls, the date of each analysis, and the results of each analysis.
8. As with all other quality control records, the CLIA requires that the records be kept for two years.

9. Each new lot of controls and/or reagents should be tested concurrently with the previous batch and *given written approval by the chief technician or laboratory director before use.*

10. Report results. The report should include:

Control values : Normal   :   seconds
              : Abnormal :   seconds
Patient values : Patient   :   seconds

11. The heating block temperature must be checked and recorded twice a day (morning and afternoon). The thermometer used to check the temperature of the block must be periodically calibrated with an NBS thermometer.

chapter nine

Quality Control in Medical Microbiology

Quality control in microbiology is difficult to contend with because of its nature. This is attributable, in part, to the diversity of media, reagents, and chemicals used in the discipline, coupled with the inherent variations of the test subject, the microorganism.

In an attempt to create a usable guide, the authors refer the reader to the excellent references (21–27) found in the bibliography. It is strongly suggested that the reader supplement this part of the manual with at least one of the references.

To prevent this portion of the text from becoming redundant, the reader is referred to Chapter 4, Equipment Maintenance. A complete program of quality control in medical microbiology consists of daily controls on the instruments and the equipment used to perform the analyses. Examples of preventive maintenance record-keeping forms are set forth in Tables 1 and 2 in Chapter 4.

MEDICAL BACTERIOLOGY

Stock Cultures

The bacteriology laboratory must maintain a collection of stock cultures to check media, stains, and reagents before use in bacteriological procedures. All personnel should be made familiar with the procedures for maintaining the cultures.

Stock Culture and Its Use   A stock culture is defined as a strain of bacteria that can be expected to perform in a reproducible manner and that conforms to certain biochemical, morphological, and serological characteristics.

Acquiring a Stock Culture Collection   The bacteria listed in the tables in this chapter may be obtained from:

1. The American Type Culture Collection (ATCC), 12301 Parklawn Drive, Rockville, Maryland 20852. (This is a private agency that maintains a wide collection of stock organisms. A catalog is available on request. It is necessary to indicate the intended use of the requested culture in order to obtain an appropriate strain.) This is the most reliable but the most expensive source ($50.00 each).
2. Proficiency-testing cultures from the Center for Disease Control serve as a source of stock cultures. These microorganisms already have been checked for their morphological, biochemical, physiological, and serological characteristics. Use caution here: these strains often are selected because they are *atypical*.
3. Isolates from pathological material. Use caution here: the characteristics may change over time causing undesirable control results.
4. Commercial sources. For the small laboratory, these dried discs represent a convenient and relatively inexpensive means of maintaining a culture collection. Average cost per pack of discs is $35.00.

Subculturing Stock Cultures   *Never* use growth directly from a stored stock culture to test the quality of a medium or to check the biochemical test or to perform any quality control procedure. An actively growing culture is needed; therefore, subculture the stock culture to a broth medium and incubate 18–24 hours. Any good infusion broth may be used for this purpose. A loopful of the broth culture may then be used for quality control testing.

A Practical Method for Preserving Stock Cultures   Stock culture preservation ranges from the highly expensive use of liquid nitrogen, to lyophilization, to the purchase of commercial organisms, to the very inexpensive method of sterile mineral oil overlay. The method used in this laboratory and described on p. 67 may be too time-consuming for a small laboratory. To compensate for this, the authors offer the mineral oil overlay technique for preserving stock cultures:

1. Purchase USP, liquid petrolatum, heavy; No. 22–88–51, Parke, Davis & Co., Detroit, Michigan.
2. Sterilize desired volumes at 170°C in a hot air oven for one hour.
3. To actively growing cultures on heart infusion agar slants (short slant, deep butt), add sterile room temperature mineral oil. The oil should rise ½ inch above the tip of the slant to prevent evaporation of medium water.
4. To retrieve the culture, use a sterile loop or needle. Drain the oil from the culture on the needle by gently touching the inner wall of the tube.

5. Inoculate the culture into Trypticase soy broth to revive for testing media.

The authors have maintained certain organisms by this method for up to five years.

Maintaining Stock Cultures in the Authors' Laboratory (Three Sets of Identical Organisms)

Set #1. Maintain Set #1 at −60°C in quick freeze tubes in sterile, defibrinated rabbit blood or on heart infusion agar covered with sterile mineral oil. A complete record of the morphology and biochemical pattern of each organism must be kept in a separate file in the laboratory. This set will serve as a reference set for Sets #2 and #3, and should rarely have to be used.

Set #2. Maintain Set #2 in the dark at room temperature in carbohydrate-free motility medium. These cultures should be transferred every two months.

Set #3. Maintain Set #3 on heart infusion agar slants. They are identical to Set #2, and they are to be used for every-day testing. These cultures must be transferred to fresh heart infusion agar slants every month. Store in the dark at room temperature.

Dehydrated Media: Control During Preparation

Good manufacturing practices are required for every facet of production from the time the raw material is first received until the time the finished product leaves the plant. Briefly, key ingredients, such as protein hydrolysates, are performance-assayed before inclusion in media formulations because of possible variations of source material and treatment.

The sources of all ingredients are recorded, the steps and conditions of manufacture are specified, followed, and documented. Finally, the manufacturer subjects the finished project to a performance test to demonstrate that the ingredients, steps, and conditions of manufacture have produced a product that meets its labeled claims and exhibits a level of performance comparable to previously manufactured lots of that product.

Adherence to specifications will minimize physical deterioration, and performance testing will validate product efficacy.

Labeling requirements include a requirement for an extensive leaflet containing full instructions for use. It provides a vehicle for supplying much more information about a product than would ordinarily be placed on a container label.

The foregoing statement was made by David Power, Ph.D., Manager, Technical Services, BioQuest, and reproduced with his written permission.

The preparation of media by laboratory personnel is becoming a dying art. The heavy reliance on commercially prepared media lures microbiologists into a false sense of security concerning the reliability of the product. As Dr. Power points out, commercial quality control is extensive; however, the manufacturer has very little control over the conditions to which laboratorians subject the media before its use. It remains the responsibility of the laboratory to ensure the reliability of the product.

The quality assurance of media prepared from dehydrated products is usually given little, if any, attention. It is the authors' recommendation that media preparation by laboratory personnel be controlled as follows:

1. Water.
   A daily check of the pH and conductivity of the distilled water used to reconstitute dehydrated media is essential. The pH should range between 5.8–7.0 and conductivity should be 10.0 μmhos or less. Periodically, the laboratory would be wise to submit a water sample for analysis of dissolved metallic ions. The water is considered acceptable if the metals exist in concentrations of less than 0.01 ppm. If conductivity and pH are found to be high, the still may need cleaning (refer to p. 16), or a demineralizer may need to be installed. Determination of amine concentration also would be useful. Monthly checks for microbial contamination are required by the College of American Pathologists.

2. Opened dehydrated products.
   If possible, purchase dehydrated media in quantities suitable to last no more than three months. Assign a date-received and date-opened tag to each bottle. If there are any visible signs of deterioration, discard the bottle. At all times, keep the media tightly sealed and *follow the manufacturers' instructions for storage and reconstitution*.

3. Sterilization.
   Do not over- or understerilize the media. Again, *follow the instructions to the letter*. Set aside a small amount of media for pH after sterilization. Conduct daily checks on sterilization temperatures and jacket/chamber pressure. Record the results of each check. Conduct monthly checks of sterilization efficiency using killit ampules.

4. pH.
   After the media has been sterilized and cooled to room temperature, check the pH of the media. Any properly operating pH meter will suffice. Most dehydrated containers list the acceptable pH range after sterilization. *If the pH varies from prescribed limits, discard the batch.*

Record the results of all pH determinations on dehydrated media along with the lot number of the media and the batch number which you assign to it.

5. After preparation.
   Do not incubate plates as a sterility check, then turn around and use them for a specimen.

Media: Control after Preparation

The shelf-life of media varies from lot to lot and medium to medium. Every batch of media should be tested before use for its ability to perform as designed. When a freshly prepared batch of media is used, it is wise to perform positive and negative control tests on each batch.

1. Differential and inhibitory media.
   These should be checked for their ability to show the characteristic, different growth and to selectively inhibit or reduce the growth of specific organisms.
2. Sterility.
   The sterility of all types of media can be checked by incubating five plates or tubes picked at random from a batch.
3. Quality control records.
   Such records are to be kept on each medium.
4. Expected results.
   Table 10 lists the control organisms used in the authors' laboratory and the expected reactions. This laboratory does not tolerate deviations from expected results. If a medium does not perform to expected values, the batch is discarded.
5. Inoculation for control purposes.
   Media can be expected to perform with the smallest amount of inoculum possible. To standardize the amount of organism placed on the medium, use a calibrated loop (0.01 ml). Suspend the control organism in infusion broth and incubate until density compares to the turbidity of a 0.03 McFarland Standard. (This represents half the concentration of a 0.5 McFarland Standard used in antimicrobic sensitivity testing.) Inoculate the medium to be tested with 0.01 ml of the growth from the infusion broth.
6. Sterile defibrinated blood.
   Before use, check all blood for sterility by adding 0.2 ml of blood to 3.0 ml of Trypticase soy broth.
7. Sterile products.

Table 10. Bacteriology media control and expected reactions

Medium	Positive control organism	Positive expected result	Negative control organism	Negative expected result
Aesculin agar	*Enterobacter aerogenes*	Blackening, loss of fluorescence	*Pseudomonas aeruginosa*	No blackening; no loss of fluorescence
Alkaline peptone water	*Vibrio cholerae*	Increased number of cells		
Anaerobic blood agar base with rabbit blood, vitamin K, and hemin	*Bacteroides melaninogenicus*	Black colonies	*Clostridium hemolyticum*	Hemolysis
Bacitracin discs (A disc)	*Streptococcus pyogenes*	Zone of inhibition (15–20 mm diameter)	Non-Group A Beta *Streptococci*	No zone of inhibition
Bile medium for anaerobes	*Bacteroides fragilis*	Growth	*Clostridium perfringens*	No growth
Bismuth sulfite	*Salmonella typhimurium*	Flat black colonies with a metallic sheen	*Escherichia coli*	No growth or inhibited (pale green)
Bordet. Gengou	*Bordetella pertussis*	Raised (domex) pearly gray colonies		
Brilliant green agar	*Escherichia coli*	Clear colonies on red medium	*Salmonella enteritidis*	No growth or inhibited (yellow-green)
Buffered glycerol saline with phenol red	*Salmonella, Shigella, Escherichia coli*	Do a pour plate for each organism after inoculation, at 1-day incubation and after 2-day incubation		
Carbohydrate agar slants:				
10% dextrose	*Escherichia coli*	Acid slant (yellow)	*A. calcoaceticus var. lwoffi*	Alkaline slant (red)
10% lactose	*Escherichia coli*	Acid slant (yellow)	*Salmonella enteritidis*	Alkaline slant (red)
Carbohydrate bases: Andrade with glucose	*Escherichia coli*	Acid (pink) and gas	*Shigella sonnei*	Acid (pink), no gas
CTA with glucose	*Neisseria gonorrhoeae*	Acid (yellow)	*Neisseria catarrhalis*	No change (red)
O–F (2% casitone with glucose)	*Pseudomonas aeruginosa*	Acid (yellow)	*A. calcoaceticus var. lwoffi*	Basic (red)

Medium	Organism	Reaction	Organism	Reaction
O-F (0.5% casitone with glucose)	Escherichia coli	Open tube: acid (yellow)	Pseudomonas aeruginosa	Open tube: acid sealed tube: no change; open tube: no change; sealed tubes: no change
Cetrimide agar	Pseudomonas aeruginosa	Growth	Escherichia coli	No growth
Citrate (Simmons)	Enterobacter aerogenes	Blue slant	Escherichia coli	No change; no growth
Chocolate agar	H. influenza	Growth		
Coagulase plasma	Staphylococcus aureus	Coagulation of plasma	Salmonella epidermidis	No coagulation
Cooked meat with iron	Clostridium subterminales	Digestion, blackening	Clostridium hemolyticum	No blackening or digestion
Cysteine heart agar	Pasteurella tularensis	Transparent, small mucoid, drop-like colonies after 2–5 days		
Decarboxylases:	Salmonella enteritidis	Alkaline (purple)	Shigella flexneri	Acid (yellow)
Lysine		Alkaline (purple)		Acid (yellow)
Ornithine		Alkaline (purple)		Acid (yellow)
Arginine		Delayed-alkaline (purple)		
Dextrose broth	Beta streptococcus	Growth		
D'nase agar	Staphylococcus aureus	Clear zone around growth with addition of HCl	Escherichia coli	No clear zone produced with HCl; no iridescent zone produced with HCl
Egg yolk-agar	Clostridium novyi A.	Lipase-iridescent zone	Clostridium subterminale	No iridescent zone or white zone
EMB	Escherichia coli	Purple colonies with a green metallic sheen	Salmonella enteritidis	Colorless colonies
Flagella broth	Pseudomonas aeruginosa	Growth with polar flagellae		
Fletcher medium	Leptospira species	Growth		
Gelatin (nutrient)	Serratia marcescens	Liquefaction	Escherichia coli	No liquefaction

continued

Table 10.—*Continued*

Medium	Positive control organism	Positive expected result	Negative control organism	Negative expected result
Heart infusion agar	*Escherichia coli*	Growth		
Heart infusion agar with basic fuchsin	*Brucella abortus*	Growth	*Brucella suis*	No growth
Heart infusion agar with defibrinated sheep blood	*Beta streptococci*	Colony surrounded by a zone of complete hemolysis (clear)	*Alpha streptococci*	Colony surrounded by a zone of incomplete hemolysis (green)
Heart infusion agar with thionin	*Brucella abortus*	No growth	*Brucella suis*	Growth
Heart infusion broth	*Escherichia coli*	Growth		
Heart infusion tyrosine	*Pseudomonas aeruginosa* with "brown pigment"	Brown pigment	*Escherichia coli*	No brown pigment
Hektoen agar	*Salmonella enteritidis*	Blue green colonies with black centers	*Escherichia coli*	Orange- or salmon-colored colonies
H_2S medium for anaerobes	*Clostridium subterminale*	Browning of medium	*Bacteroides fragilis*	No browning of the medium
Indole-nitrite medium	*Propionibacterium acnes*	Indole and nitrate pos. (red reaction with the addition of reagents)	*Clostridium subterminale*	Indole and nitrate negative (no color reaction produced with the addition of test)
Iron milk	*Clostridium perfringens*	Stormy fermentation	*Bacteroides fragilis*	Clot produced
Kligler iron agar	*Salmonella enteritidis*	Basic slant (red); acid butt (yellow) with H_2S (blackening)	*Escherichia coli*	Acid slant (yellow) Acid butt (yellow)
Kligler iron agar	*Shigella flexneri*	Basic slant (red); acid butt (yellow)		
KL virulence agar	*C. diphtheriae*	Lines of precipitation	*Staphylococcus* species	No lines of precipitation
Leoffler's serum agar	*C. diphtheriae*	Luxuriant growth with typical cell morphology		

Medium	Organism	Result	Organism	Result
Leptospira medium	*Leptospira species*	Growth	*Salmonella enteritidis*	No change
Litmus milk	*Escherichia coli*	Acid	*Proteus mirabilis*	Red slant
Lysine iron agar	*Salmonella enteritidis*	Alkaline slant (purple) H_2S (blackening)		Acid butt (yellow)
McBride *Listeria* medium	*Listeria monocytogenes*	Blue-green colonies (with scanning microscope)		
MacConkey agar				
(a) plates (enteric)	*Salmonella enteritidis*	Colorless colonies	*Escherichia coli*	Pink colonies
(b) slants	*Pseudomonas aeruginosa*	Growth	*Neisseria mucosa*	No growth
Malonate broth (modified)	*Proteus mirabilis*	Blue (alkaline)	*Escherichia coli*	No change
Mannitol salt agar	*S. aureus*	Yellow colonies	*Escherichia coli*	No growth
0.4% Motility medium	*Enterobacter aerogenes*	Growth spreading out from the stab line; motile	*Shigella sonnei*	No growth away from the stab line; nonmotile
MR-VP broth	*Escherichia coli*	Red reaction with reagent	*Enterobacter aerogenes*	Yellow reaction with reagent
Mucate broth	*Escherichia coli*	Yellow-green (acid)	*Shigella sonnei*	No change (blue)
VP (Voges-Proskauer)	*Escherichia coli*	No color change	*Enterobacter aerogenes*	Red reaction with reagent
Nitrate broth	*Escherichia coli*	Red reaction with reagents	*P. aeruginosa*	No color change; gas production
special infusion	*Pseudomonas aeruginosa*	No color with reagents, gas produced	Uninoculated	No change with addition of reagents, Zn produces red reaction
Nitrite broth	*Alcaligenes odorans*	No color with reagents, gas produced	Uninoculated	Red reaction with reagents
Nutrient agar	*Neisseria mucosa*	Growth	*Neisseria gonorrhoeae*	No growth
Nutrient broth	*Pseudomonas aeruginosa*	Growth		
Nutrient broth with 6% NaCl	*Streptococcus fecalis*	Growth	*Acinetobacter*	No growth

continued

Table 10.—Continued

Medium	Positive control organism	Positive expected result	Negative control organism	Negative expected result
6.5% NaCl	Streptococcus fecalis	Growth		
ONPG disc (1,3-D-galactosidase)	Escherichia coli	Yellow color-positive	Salmonella enteritidis	No color change
Organic acids				
a) citrate	Salmonella enteritidis	Yellow (acid) with diminution of ppt. volume upon addition of 0.5 ml 50% neutral lead acetate solution (as compared to control)	Uninoculated	No change (blue)
b) tartrate	Salmonella enteritidis	Same as for citrate		
Pectate agar	Pectobacterium species	Liquefaction	Enterobacter aerogenes	No liquefaction
Phenylalanine agar	Proteus mirabilis	Green reaction with addition of 10% $FeCl_3$	Escherichia coli	No color reaction with reagent
Potassium cyanide	Enterobacter aerogenes	Growth (turbidity)	Escherichia coli	No growth
Pseudomonas agar F (fluorescent agar)	Pseudomonas aeruginosa	Greenish-yellow fluorescence	Escherichia coli	No pigment or fluorescence
Pseudomonas agar P (technicolor agar)	Pseudomonas aeruginosa	Blue pigment-fluorescence	Escherichia coli	No pigment
Salmonella Shigella agar				
a) plates (enteric)	Salmonella enteritidis	Colorless colonies	Escherichia coli	No growth or inhibited growth (pink colonies)
b) slants	Pseudomonas aeruginosa	Growth	A. calcoaceticus var. lwoffi	No growth
Selenite broth	Shigella sonnei	Survival		
Seller's differential agar	A. calcoaceticus var. lwoffi	Blue slant; no change in butt	A. calcoaceticus var. anatratum	Blue slant; yellow band; no change in butt
Sodium acetate agar	Escherichia coli	Blue (alkaline) slant	Shigella sonnei	No change (green)
Strep. fecalis broth	Streptococcus fecalis	Yellow-brown color	Beta streptococci	No change (purple)

Medium	Organism	Result	Organism	Result
TCBS (Thiosulfate citrate, Biosalts, sucrose)	V. cholerae	Yellow; convex	Salmonella	Bluish colony
Tellurite glycine agar (TGA)	Corynebacterium diphtheriae		Staphylococcus	No growth or inhibited
Tetrathionate broth with brilliant green	Salmonella	Growth occurs while coliforms inhibited	Escherichia coli	No growth or inhibited
Thayer Martin	Neisseria gonorrhoeae	Small, translucent colonies	N. catarrhalis	No growth or inhibited
Thiogel medium	Clostridium subterminale	Liquefaction of medium	Bacteroides fragilis	No liquefaction of medium
Tinsdale agar	Clostridium diphtheriae	Black colonies with black brown halos	Streptococci	No growth or inhibited (no black halo)
Transgrow medium (see protocol for checking Transgrow)				
Tryptic soy broth	Beta streptococci	Supports growth		
Triple sugar iron agar	Salmonella	Alkaline slant (red) Acid butt (yellow) Gas H_2S (blackening)	Enterobacter aerogenes	Acid slant (yellow) Acid butt (yellow) Gas No H_2S
Tryptone broth (Indole)	Escherichia coli	Red reaction with reagents	Enterobacter aerogenes	No reaction with reagents
Tryptone glucose yeast slants	Pseudomonas aeruginosa	Growth at 25°C Growth at 37°C Growth at 42°C		
Urea agar	Proteus mirabilis	Strongly positive (pink reaction)	Escherichia coli	No change
	Enterobacter aerogenes	Weakly positive (pink reaction slant)		
X factor disc	H. influenza	No growth	H. influenza	No growth
XLD agar	Shigella flexneri	Red colonies	K. pneumoniae	Inhibited (yellow colonies)

Five percent of all commercially prepared reagents labeled sterile should be incubated for 24 hours at 35°C before use or at the time the lot is received. Results must be recorded.
8. Commercial media.
   Control and document as above.

Reagents and Stains

All reagents and stains should be checked to determine their ability to perform using positive and negative controls. In the authors' laboratory, results are recorded on the form for media, stains, and reagents (Figure 6).

Antigen Typing Sera

Typing sera should be purchased from a reliable source. The antiserum must be reconstituted according to the manufacturers' instructions, and stored between 2–8°C. Known positive and negative controls are to be performed on reconstituted antiserum before use and with each batch of tests.

Fluorescent Antibody Conjugate

Conjugate should be purchased from a reliable source and used according to the manufacturers' specifications. Undiluted conjugate is stored at –60°C before use. Positive and negative controls are used to test the efficiency and reliability of the conjugate. These controls should be run with each batch of tests.

Antibiotic Susceptibility Tests

Agar Diffusion Method The well recognized standard method described by Bauer et al. should be followed (28):

1. Discs.
   Purchase discs from a reliable source. The stock supply must be stored at –20°C with a dessicant. The working supply can be stored at 5°C with a dessicant.
2. Agar.
   Mueller-Hinton agar can be prepared and poured, in 60-ml portions, into small dilution bottles and sterilized. After sterilization, the agar is cooled to 45°C and poured. Unused plates can be safely stored at 5°C in plastic bags up to seven days. Discard after seven days. If a precipitate is visible, discard the plates.

RECORD OF
QUALITY CONTROL FOR MEDIA

Medium or reagent _____

Date prepared	Tested	Lot number	Final pH	Sterility 25°C 35°C	Performance and organism	Initials of technician

Figure 6. Sample form used to record results of quality control testing for media, stains, and reagents.

3. Inoculum.

Grow the organism in Trypticase soy broth or diluted to a turbidity comparable to a 0.5 McFarland Standard. The standard should be prepared each month. Comparative turbidity with this standard places the organism in the log phase of its growth cycle where it is most susceptible to the deleterious effect of the antibiotics. Store the

McFarland Standard at room temperature in the dark. Make certain that the container is tightly sealed.

4. Inoculating and Incubation.
   Two directional swab methods (28).

5. Reading and Interpretation.
   All zones are measured in millimeters across the transverse aspect of the zone, and the results are recorded on the appropriate forms (Figure 7). A record should be kept of each organism's susceptibility pattern for future reference.

6. Controls.
   Precision and accuracy of the discs must be measured with each batch of tests using the strains *Escherichia coli* ATCC 25922, *Staphylococcus aureus* ATCC 25923, and *Pseudomonas aeruginosa* ATCC 27853. Results must be recorded. Acceptable zone sizes are listed in Table 11.

QUALITY CONTROL FORM
Antibiotic Disc Susceptibility

Date _____   Disc _____

	E. coli ATCC 25922		S. aureus ATCC 25923		Pseudomonas ATCC 27853		Enterococcus	
Allowable limits (mm)								
Day	Zone	Disc Lot No.	Zone	Disc Lot No.	Zone	Disc Lot No.	Zone	Disc Lot No.
1								
2								
3								
4								
5								
6								
7								
8								
9								
10								
11								
12								
13								
14								
15								
16								
17								
18								
19								
20								
21								
22								
23								
24								
25								
26								
27								
28								
29								
30								
31								

Figure 7. Sample form used to record results from the agar diffusion method of antibiotic susceptibility testing.

Table 11. Acceptable zone size ranges, disc diffusion test[a]

Antibiotic	Disc content	Zone size (mm)		
		E. coli (ATCC 25922)	S. aureus (ATCC 25923)	P. aeruginosa (ATCC 27853)
Ampicillin	10 μg	15–20	24–35	
Carbenicillin	100 μg	24–29	N.A.	19–25[b]
Cephalothin	30 μg	18–23	25–37	
Chloramphenicol	30 μg	21–27	19–26	
Clindamycin	2 μg	N.A.	23–29	
Erythromycin	15 μg	8–14	22–30	
Gentamycin	10 μg	19–26	19–27	16–22[b]
Kanamycin	30 μg	17–25	19–26	
Methicillin	5 μg	N.A.	17–22	
Neomycin	30 μg	17–23	18–26	
Penicillin G	10 units	N.A.	26–37	
Polymyxin B	300 units	12–16	7–13	13–18[b]
Streptomycin	10 μg	12–20	14–22	
Tetracycline	30 μg	18–25	19–28	
Tobramycin	10 μg	18–26	19–29	19–25
Trimethroprim	1.25 μg			
Sulfamethoxazole	23.75 μg	24–32	24–32	
Vancomycin	30 μg	N.A.	15–19	

[a]National Committee for Clinical Laboratory Standards–ASM-2, Performance Standards for Antimicrobial Disc Susceptibility Tests. Reproduced with written permission of NCCLS, Villanova, Pennsylvania.

[b]Modified ranges recommended by C. Thornsberry, Ph.D. Antimicrobial Susceptibility Testing Unit, Center for Disease Control, Atlanta, Georgia.

N.A. = not applicable.

7. New Discs.
   Determine the ability of new lots of susceptibility discs to perform when they arrive in the laboratory by repeating Procedure 6.
   Minimal Inhibitory Concentration Test For this test, follow the procedure described below:

1. Use only pure antimicrobial powders. Store the powders at −60°C under dessication.
2. Weigh the powders to four decimal places and establish a standard

dilution scheme that encompasses the clinically useful concentrations of drugs.
3. Once a working solution is thawed, it should not be refrozen and thawed again.

Anaerobes

Anaerobic techniques and materials should be controlled in much the same manner as are facultative or aerobic materials (described previously).

In anaerobic quality control, the analyst should give special consideration to the following points:

1. Stock cultures.

   The spore formers (*Bacillus* or *Clostridium* species) keep well on brain heart infusion agar at 5°C if the tubes are tightly sealed. The nonspore formers (*Bacteroides* species) should probably be kept on a carbohydrate-free, semi-solid medium (motility medium) at 5°C. These organisms will have to be transferred weekly.

2. Anaerobic system.

   It is imperative that each Brewer jar contain a redox indicator (methylene blue oxygen indicator), as well as a stock culture known to be oxygen intolerant, plated on an appropriate media, and incubated in the same system with the test specimens.

MYCOBACTERIOLOGY

A list of the biochemical tests and the positive and negative controls used in the authors' laboratory is set forth in Table 12. In addition to quality

Table 12. Suggested controls in mycobacteriology

Biochemical	Positive control	Negative control
Niacin	H37RV	*M. fortuitum*
Nitrate reduction	H37RV	*M. aquae*
Catalase 68C	*M. aquae*	H37RV
Tween 80 degradation	*M. kansassi*	*M. intracellulare*
Tellurite reduction	*M. fortuitum*	*M. aquae*
5% NaCl	*M. fortuitum*	*M. aquae*
Wayne's arysulfatase	*M. fortuitum*	*M. aquae*
MacConkeys'	*M. fortuitum*	*M. aquae*
Urease	*M. fortuitum*	*M. aquae*
L-J medium	*M. tuberculosis*	
7H-10 medium	*M. tuberculosis*	

control of media, the analyst is urged to consult the Center for Disease Control for the proper methods of care and maintenance of the Biological Safety Cabinet. Mycobacteriology should not be practiced without the use of a Biological Safety Cabinet which has an airflow across the face of the hood of less than 50 feet per minute. Ultraviolet lights need to be checked for intensity and filters need to be changed periodically (29).

MEDICAL MYCOLOGY

Media and Reagents

Before Use Check each batch of media and reagents for proper pH, sterility, and ability to perform as designed (refer to p. 84). Performance is assayed by inoculating the medium to be evaluated with the appropriate fungus or bacterium and recording the results on the Media/Reagent

Table 13. Mycology quality control organisms

Actinomycetes:
  Nocardia asteroides
  Streptomyces species
Bacteria:
  Escherichia coli
  Staphylococcus aureus
Molds:
  Blastomyces dermatitidis
  Cladosporium werneckii
  Histoplasma capsulatum
  Microsporum canis
  Scopulariopsis brevicaulis
  Trichophyton rubrum
  Trichophyton tonsurans
  Trichophyton verrucosum
Yeasts:
  Candida albicans
  Candida pseudotropicalis
  Candida tropicalis
  Cryptococcus laurentii
  Cryptococcus neoformans
  Cryptococcus terreus
  Torulopsis glabrata

Table 14. Quality control expected reactions for yeast fermentation

Carbohydrate with yeast nitrogen base	Gas production	No gas production
Galactose	*Candida pseudotropicalis*	*Cryptococcus laurentii*
Glucose	*Candida tropicalis*	*Cryptococcus laurentii*
Lactose	*Candida pseudotropicalis*	*Cryptococcus laurentii*
Maltose	*Candida tropicalis*	*Cryptococcus laurentii*
Sucrose	*Candida tropicalis*	*Cryptococcus laurentii*
Trehalose	*Torulopsis glabrata*	*Cryptococcus laurentii*

Quality Control Check List (Figure 6). All other pertinent information on the check list is completed before the media are utilized.

Storage Conditions Unless otherwise indicated by the manufacturer, all prepared media and reagents are stored at 5°C and preferably utilized in one month. Each medium is given an expiration date, and quantities of media are ordered to coincide with usage rate and expiration dates.

Expected Reactions A list of media, reagents, and stock cultures used in mycology quality control and their abilities to perform as designed are provided in Tables 14, 15, 16, and 17.

Stock Cultures

(Refer to Table 13.)

Mycology Stock Culture Collection Establish a collection of catalogued fungi. These organisms should be used for reference, evaluation of media, training, and proficiency testing.

Mycology Culture Collection Data Assign each organism a permanent accession number after its morphology and biochemical pattern have been established.

Maintenance of Stock Cultures The method outlined below is used in the authors' laboratory.

1. Yeasts (each isolate):
     Set #1. Inoculate molds on Orr's freezing agar or Sabouraud's, incu-
          for 72 hours, and then frozen at −20°C.
     Set #2. Yeasts are dispensed into 1-dram vials containing sterile, distilled, demineralized water. A heavy suspension is made in each vial. They can be stored at room temperature and are the working cultures.
2. Molds (each isolate):
     Set #1. Inoculate molds on Orr's freezing agar or Sabouraud's, incu-

Table 15. Quality control expected reactions for yeast assimilation

Carbohydrate with yeast nitrogen base plus 2% Nobles agar	Assimilation (growth)	No assimilation (no growth)
Erythritol	*Cryptococcus laurentii*	*Candida krusei*
Galactose	*Cryptococcus laurentii*	*Candida krusei*
Glucose	*Cryptococcus laurentii*	*Candida krusei*
Inositol	*Cryptococcus laurentii*	*Candida krusei*
Lactose	*Cryptococcus laurentii*	*Cryptococcus neoformans*
Maltose	*Cryptococcus laurentii*	*Candida krusei*
Melezitose	*Cryptococcus laurentii*	*Candida krusei*
Melibiose	*Cryptococcus laurentii*	*Candida krusei*
Raffinose	*Cryptococcus laurentii*	*Candida krusei*
Sucrose	*Cryptococcus laurentii*	*Candida krusei*
Trehalose	*Cryptococcus laurentii*	*Candida krusei*
Xylose	*Cryptococcus laurentii*	*Candida krusei*

bate at 25°C until adequate growth is observed, and then freeze at −20°C.

Set #2. Inoculate selected dermatophytes on an appropriate medium and incubate at 25°C. These organisms can be kept at room temperature for approximately one month before being transferred to fresh medium.

Set #3. Transfer conidia and hyphal fragments from actively sporulating cultures and place the fragments in 1-dram vials of sterile, distilled, demineralized water. The vials can also be maintained at room temperature.

3. Media and reagent storage codes:

a. Media:

All media used in mycology for the identification of pathogenic fungi can be stored at 5°C.

b. Reagents:

A list of all reagents, chemicals, and stains used in mycology appears in Table 18 of this manual. A storage code is assigned each medium and/or reagent for information when receiving reagents in the authors' laboratory. The storage code is a simple method for cataloging the appropriate conditions in which the materials are to be stored. While this system is not necessary, we have found it to be beneficial for setting up and retrieving materials in this area.

Table 16. Mycology media control and expected reactions

Media	Expected positive reaction	Positive control	Negative control
Casein agar	Hydrolysis: Zone of clearing around colony	Streptomyces	Nocardia asteroides
Orr's freezing agar	Enhancement of sporulation; storage of cultures at 26°C	Scopulariopsis brevicaulis	N.A.
Corn meal agar with Tween 80	Chlamydospore formation	Candida albicans	N.A.
Dermatophyte test medium	Red color change of agar	Trichophyton rubrum	N.A.
12% Gelatin medium	Liquefaction of gelatin	Cladosporium werneckii	N.A.
Kelly's agar	Conversion of Blastomyces mold form to yeast form	Blastomyces dermatitidis	N.A.
Mycobiotic agar	Inhibition of yeast growth caused by cycloheximide	Torulopsis glabrata	N.A.
Nitrate Test with yeast nitrogen base	Growth	Cryptococcus terreus	Cryptococcus laurentii
Potato dextrose agar	Refer to Orr's freezing agar		
Rice grains	Yellow pigment	Microsporum canis	Microsporum audouinii

Sabhi agar	Enrichment for isolation	*Scopulariopsis brevicaulis*	N.A.
Sabouraud dextrose agar (4.0%)	Typical colonial morphology and reverse pigmentation	*Trichophyton rubrum*	N.A.
Sabouraud dextrose broth	Sterility check and growth	*Candida albicans*	N.A.
Sabouraud dextrose agar with Thiamine	Enhance growth of some dermatophytes	*Trichophyton tonsurans*	N.A.
Tyrosine agar	Hydrolysis: Zone of clearing	*Streptomyces*	*Nocardia asteroides*
Urea agar	Reddening of agar surface	*Cryptococcus laurentii*	*Torulopsis glabrata*
Xanthine agar	Hydrolysis: Zone of clearing	*Streptomyces*	*Nocardia asteroides*
Bird seed agar	Brown to black pigmentation	*Cryptococcus neoformans*	*Cryptococcus laurentii*
Czapek solution agar	Good sporulation	*Scopulariopsis brevicaulis*	N.A.
Malt extract agar	Rapid growth	*Scopulariopsis brevicaulis*	N.A.
Trichophyton agars (1–4)	Enhancement of growth	*Trichophyton tonsurans; Trichophyton verrucosum*	*Trichophyton mentagrophytes*
Brain heart infusion agar with streptomycin and penicillin	Inhibit bacterial growth	*Staphylococcus aureus*	N.A.
V-8 juice agar	Stimulate ascospore production	*Saccharomyces cerevisiae*	N.A.

Table 17. Mycology reagent control and expected reactions

Stain or reagent	Expected result	Positive	Negative
Absolute alcohol	N.A.	N.A.	N.A.
Gram stain	Stain bacterial wall	Staphylococcus (blue color)	E. coli (red color)
Acetone alcohol	Decolorization, refer to gram stain		
1% crystal violet	Primary stain, refer to gram stain		
Iodine-gram stain Burke	Mordant, refer to gram stain		
Kinyoun's acid fast stain	Red organism if acid fast	Nocardia asteroides	N.A.
India ink	N.A.	Periodically check the stain to assure the absence of any contaminating organism such as Candida	

N.A. = not applicable.

Table 18. Reagent storage conditions

Reagent	Container	Storage temperature	Expiration date	Code
Toluene	metal	25°C	N.S.	M-25-N.S.
Xylene	metal or glass	25°C	N.S.	M/G-25-N.S.
Amphyl	metal can	25°C	N.S.	M-25-N.S.
In HCl	glass	25°C	N.S.	G-25-N.S.
Sugars (powder)	polyethylene	25°C dry environment	1 year	Poly-25-1 year
KNO$_3$	polyethylene	25°C dry environment	N.S.	Poly-25-N.S.
DAP	glass	25°C dry environment	6 months	G-25-6 months
Phthalic acid	glass	25°C dry environment	6 months	G-25-6 months
Ninhydrin	glass	25°C dry environment	6 months	G-25-6 months
Peptone	polyethylene	25°C dry environment	1 year	Poly-25-1 year
Trypticase	polyethylene	25°C dry environment	1 year	Poly-25-1 year
Saline (0.85%)	glass	25°C dry environment	6 months	G-5-6 months
Water	glass	5°C	6 months	G-5-6 months
Basic fuchsin	brown bottle	25°C	3 months	BB-25-3 months
Periodic acid	brown bottle	25°C	fresh	BB-25-F
Sodium meta bisulfite	brown bottle	25°C	fresh	BB-25-F
Permount	brown bottle	25°C	1 year	BB-25-1 year
Formalin	glass	25°C	N.S.	G-25-N.S.
Crystal violet	brown bottle	25°C	N.S.	BB-25-N.S.
Kinyouns	brown bottle	25°C	N.S.	BB-25-N.S.
Immersion oil	brown bottle	25°C	N.S.	BB-25-N.S.

continued

Table 18.—*Continued*

Reagent	Container	Storage temperature	Expiration date	Code
Na_2CO_3	glass	5°C	6 months	G-5-6 months
10% Na_2CO_3	glass	5°C	6 months	G-5-6 months
1% H_2SO_4	glass	25°C	6 months	G-25-6 months
5% Na_2CO_3	glass	5°C	6 months	G-5-6 months
KH_2PO_4	glass	5°C	6 months	G-5-6 months
Acetone	glass or metal	25°C	N.S.	G/M-25-N.S.
Gram's iodine	brown bottle	25°C	N.S.	BB-5-N.S.
Albumin fixative	brown bottle	5°C	N.S.	BB-5-1 year
Mercurochrom	brown bottle	25°C	N.S.	BB-25-N.S.
5% Na_2CO_3	glass	5°C	6 months	G-5-6 months
Na citrate solution	glass	5°C	6 months	G-5-6 months
M/15 phosphate buffer	glass	5°C	3 months	G-5-3 months
N-acetyl-l-cysteine	glass	5°C	1 month	G-5-1 month
Ba (OH)$_2$ saturated	glass	25°C	N.S.	G-25-N.S.
6 N HCl	glass	25°C	N.S.	G-25-N.S.
1N H_2SO_4	glass	25°C	N.S.	G-25-N.S.
Pyridine	brown bottle	25°C	N.S.	BB-25-N.S.
Methanol	brown bottle	25°C	N.S.	BB-25-N.S.
Butyl alcohol	brown bottle	25°C	N.S.	BB-25-N.S.

N.S. = none stated in the literature.

PARASITOLOGY

In parasitology, the analyst is beset by a somewhat less well defined and less rigid guideline for quality control techniques. It is essential, however, that checks and monitoring be undertaken to ensure a satisfactory level of performance in diagnosis. The reader is referred to reference 30 which may be obtained by writing to the Center for Disease Control. The following information in this section was adapted for use with written permission from the Center for Disease Control, Parasitology Training Branch.

Equipment

Microscopes The microscope is perhaps the most important piece of equipment used in parasitology. The following precautions and measures need to be taken to meet recommended standards:

1. Objective:
   low power (10X, 16 mm); high dry (40–45X, 4 mm); oil immersion (97–100X, 1.8 mm)
2. Oculars:
   10X and 5X
3. Calibrated ocular micrometer
4. Adjustable substage condenser with regulatory iris diaphragm
5. Adequate illumination:
   a. Built-in—with a voltage regulator and filters
   b. Separate—with a condensing system, regulatory iris diaphragm, and maneuverability
6. Care of the microscope:
   Keep the microscope clean and free from dust. Surface lenses of both objectives and oculars should be cleaned frequently with a high quality lens paper. A good quality, *low viscosity*, immersion oil is essential. Cedar, mineral, or similar oils damage the microscope and the slide preparations.
7. Calibration of micrometer:
   Refer to reference 30.

Centrifuge Any explosion-proof model which meets the following criteria can be considered acceptable:

1. Equipped to handle 15-ml, conical, centrifuge tubes, or 100 X 13 mm tubes.
2. Calibrated with a tachometer and marked at the settings for the RPM routinely used. (Refer to Preventive Maintenance in Chapter 4.) (Note: Angle-head centrifuges are unsatisfactory for parasitology specimens.)

Exhaust Hood The laboratory must perform formalin-ether extraction in an exhaust hood with a suitable air intake velocity. The minimal and maximal safe limits of air velocity have been established to be between 50–150 linear feet/minute (29). Periodic inspection of the air velocity can be accomplished with a velometer.

Refrigerator An explosion-proof refrigerator is essential because ether will be stored in it if the formalin-ether procedure is used. The temperature should be approximately 5°C and monitored twice daily.

Procedures

Preparing Wet Mounts Too thick or too thin preparations reduce the accuracy and reliability of diagnosis. To reduce the possibility of contamination of stock solutions, add the drop of mounting fluid to the slide before adding the feces.

Preparing Concentrations Control the amount of sediment obtained in both the initial and the final centrifugations.

Staining Timing of the various stages of staining and destaining is essential. Slides should be drained of excess solution between steps in the staining procedure. Keep the stain dishes covered at all times to prevent the dehydrating solutions from absorbing moisture from the air.

Solutions

Saline Replace with fresh saline every 2–3 months. Check frequently for contamination.

Iodine (1%) Replace with fresh iodine every 10–14 days. If Lugol's iodine is used, dilute 1:5 with saline. Replace with fresh Lugol's every 10–14 days.

Zinc Sulfate Check specific gravity at the time of preparation and at 1–2-month intervals to assure proper density for floating organisms. The correct specific gravity should be 1.18 for fresh fecal specimens. Adjust with water or zinc sulfate to obtain the required density. A specific gravity of 1.2 is required for formalinized specimens.

Staining Solutions:

1. Hematoxylin (0.5%):
   Very unstable. Prepare fresh daily.
2. Trichrome:
   Stable. Replace when staining becomes poor as evidenced by a check with a control slide.
3. Iron-alum:
   Replace with fresh solution every 2–3 days.

Reference Materials

Known Positives Known positive reference specimens should be used for comparison with unknown organisms when needed. Refer to reference 30, Preservation of Specimens, p. 59.

Kodachrome Slides Purchased from several commercial sources. Refer to reference 30, p. 185. These slides can be used as training aids.

Another source of specimen reference materials is the Biological Center, Inc. 6780 Jackson Road, Ann Arbor, Michigan 48103.

chapter ten

Quality Control in Immunology and Syphilis Serology

Quality control is discussed here by listing the more common tests usually performed in a clinical hospital laboratory and by pointing out precautions for each test.

Weekly thermometer calibration is recommended because times and incubation temperatures are of critical importance in this area. Daily records of water bath temperatures are mandatory. Refer to Chapter 4, Equipment Maintenance, for methods of determining hot spots in water baths.

SEROLOGICAL TESTS FOR SYPHILIS

VDRL Slide Flocculation Tests

(Supplement this section with reference 31.)

Sera All sera must be examined when removed from the water bath and those specimens containing particulate debris are to be recentrifuged. Hemolyzed sera may give false positive results; therefore, testing of hemolyzed sera should be prohibited. Also, sera to be tested more than four hours after the original heating period must be reheated at 56°C for 10 minutes.

Slides New slides should be cleaned with sulfuric acid-potassium dichromate cleaning solution, rinsed repeatedly in hot running tap water, and finally rinsed in distilled water. Slides in continual use should be cleaned in sulfuric acid-potassium dichromate solution at least once a week.

Antigen Emulsion

Preparation of Antigen Emulsion Antigen must be added drop by drop to the VDRL-buffered saline solution, but rapidly enough so that

93

approximately six seconds are allowed for each 0.5 ml of antigen addition. The pipette tip should remain in the upper third of the bottle and rotation should not be vigorous enough to splash saline onto the pipette.

Testing Antigen Emulsion Delivery Needles It is of primary importance that the proper amount of antigen emulsion be used, and for this reason the needle used must be checked each day for accuracy of delivery. Care must be exercised to obtain drops of constant size.

Preliminary Testing of Antigen Emulsion Each preparation of antigen emulsion must first be examined by testing sera of known quantitative reactivity in the "reactive," "weakly reactive," and "nonreactive" zones. Serum controls of graded reactivity must be included during a testing period to ensure proper reactivity of antigen emulsion at the time tests are performed.

Quantitative VDRLs must follow a positive qualitative slide test.

Rapid Plasma Reagin Test

This must be performed with the ambient temperature between 22–30°C (VDRL also).

Dispenser Once the bottle has been filled with the antigen from the ampule, the expiration date of the antigen changes to three months. The expiration date on the sealed ampule is no longer valid. Note that the expiration date on the dispensing bottle can never exceed that of the sealed ampule. In addition to the above, it is wise to thoroughly rinse, clean, and dry the dispenser before the addition of the new antigen.

Delivery Needle The antigen delivery needle should deliver 60 drops ± 2 drops of antigen suspension per ml. To check the accuracy of delivery, proceed as follows:

1. Attach the needle to a 2.0-ml syringe.
2. Hold the needle and syringe in a *vertical position*.
3. Allow 0.5 ml of suspension to dispense from the syringe, and count the number of drops as delivery is underway.
4. If 30 drops ± 1 drop are delivered to 0.5 ml, the needle is accurate. If not, discard the needle.
5. Record these results on a daily basis.

Antigen Test each ampule of antigen in parallel with the previous ampule before use. Record the results of the parallel testing. Control sera of known graded activity must be tested each day before use and results properly recorded. All antigens must be stored at a temperature between 2–8°C.

Test Card To prevent buckling, keep the cards flat, dry, covered, and never allow the inner circles to be touched.

Controls Prepare or purchase a nonreactive serum control, a minimally reactive serum control, and a reactive serum control. Preparation of the controls is described in reference 31. The titer of both reactive sera must be known and verified by titration on a monthly basis. The controls must be run with each batch of tests.

RAPID LATEX AGGLUTINATION TEST
FOR DETERMINATION OF ANTISTREPTOLYSIN "O"(ASO)

Serum

The serum must be free of hemolysis and debris.

Card Rotator Speed

The rotator RPM must be calibrated and set at 150 RPM each day of use.

Titer

The reaction must be read immediately. In certain cases of greatly increased ASO titer (more than 2,000 IU/ml), agglutination may be inhibited because of a prozone effect. When this is suspected, dilute the patient's serum 1:4 with sterile N (0.85%) saline and repeat the procedure.

Storage of Reagents

Store all test reagents at 2–8°C. *Do not freeze.* Reconstituted Streptolysin "O" must be discarded after use. When reconstituting Streptolysin "O," reconstitute with cold distilled water, avoiding aeration and harsh mixing. The reagent must be kept on ice at all times to avoid oxidation.

Controls

Perform the procedure and record positive and negative controls with each batch of tests.

SLIDE TEST FOR INFECTIOUS MONONUCLEOSIS (ORTHO
DIAGNOSTICS): POSITIVE CONTROL AND CONTROL TESTING

The Ortho positive control was selected for its "weak positive" reaction. This serum must be used to check the reagents upon arrival in the laboratory and to check the sensitivity of the test procedure on a daily basis. Perform test, examine, and record as above.

RAPID SLIDE TEST FOR RHEUMATOID FACTOR

Controls

RA-Test positive and negative controls may be purchased or prepared. To prepare a positive control, dilute reactive human serum 1:20. For a negative control, dilute normal human serum 1:20.

Storage

All reagents and controls must be stored between 2–8°C. The reagents must be brought to room temperature before use.

Interpretation of Test Results

All results must be compared with the control sera.

1. Negative (nonreactive) Control:
   Smooth suspension with no visible flocculation
2. Weakly Reactive Control:
   Visible flocculation with small aggregates
3. Reactive Control:
   Visible flocculation with large aggregates and a clear background

COMPLEMENT FIXATION TESTS

Each batch of specimens must include a serum complement control, an antigen complement control, and a complement diluent control. The serum complement control should consist of sensitized cells, doubling dilutions of patient's serum, and complement. The antigen complement control should consist of sensitized cells, antigen, and complement. The results of the controls must be recorded with each run.

In addition to the above, an erythrocyte control (sensitized cells and buffer) must be included and results recorded with each batch of tests. Standardization of the erythrocyte suspension must be accomplished before each test. The spectrophotometric method usually is preferred to centrifugation.

Each new vial of hemolysin must be titrated before use. Results of reactions must be recorded.

With each batch of specimens, i.e., before each test, the complement must be titrated and the results of the titration properly recorded. Antigen back titration must be accomplished with each new lot of antigen.

As with all other controls each new lot of control must be tested in parallel with the previous lot before its use. The results of the control reactions must be properly recorded. Reference 32 is a comprehensive guide to the performance of complement fixation tests.

IMMUNODIAGNOSTIC QUALITATIVE
PREGNANCY TEST PROCEDURE (PREGNOSTICON ACCUSPHERES)

Urine

It is preferable to use the first voided urine after arising in the morning. Bloody urine, or urines that have been frozen or stored for several days, give unsatisfactory results.

Filter Paper or Centrifuge

Centrifugation is preferred because certain brands of filter paper bind the hormone (HCG). If centrifugation is impossible, use Whatman #4 Filter Paper. It is the least adsorptive.

Reading Test Results

If the urine is from a pregnant female, a definite clear-cut brown ring appears within two hours in the bottom of the test tube. An ill-defined, irregular, or broken ring indicates that the sediment has been disturbed and that the test should be repeated. *Do not report as negative* before two hours.

Important Points on Technique

The following techniques should be observed in testing:

1. When measuring or adding any of the fluids used in the test, use only measuring pipettes (serological pipettes).
2. Avoid the use of soaps or detergents to clean the pipettes because traces of detergent can have a detrimental effect on the end point.
3. Positive and Negative Controls (purchased from the company or from a positive and negative specimen on a previous run) must be tested concurrently with the specimens and properly recorded.
4. In any type of kit test, it is wise to follow the manufacturer's packaged instructions to the letter.

Interference

The following drugs and pathological conditions may result in a false positive test with any kit:

1. Drug:
   Methadone .... 10–140 mg/day
   Chlorpromazine .... 50–1,200 mg/day
   Haloperidol .... 2–20 mg/day
   Thioridazine .... 50–500 mg/day
2. Pathological Conditions:
   Proteinuria
   Others–Consult reference 7.

chapter eleven
Quality Control in Urinalysis

PROCEDURE MANUAL

In addition to the guidelines mentioned on p. 3, the procedure manual for urinalysis should include:

1. A detailed description of procedures for microscopic analysis and dipstick screening. Quantitative or qualitative confirmatory tests must be used to confirm a positive dipstick.
2. The speed of centrifugation for each test
3. Materials that are to be used in each step of the procedure, to include reagents, solutions, strips, or tablets
4. A complete description of controls used to ensure the accuracy of test results

CONTROLS

Several lyophilized urine controls are commercially available for checking dipsticks. If the laboratory cannot justify the price of the commercial controls, the authors offer a receipe for preparing an in-house dipstick control:

Method of Preparation of Control Urine
1. To 100.0 ml of 0.85% sterile saline aseptically add the following: 1) 0.2 ml of sterile lysed red blood cells, 2) 0.2 ml of the sterile saturated glucose solution, 3) 0.2 ml of acetone, 4) 1.0 ml of a sterile 4% Bovalbumin solution, and 5) 2.0 ml of a sterile bilirubin solution. (To prepare the bilirubin solution, add 1.06 g of sodium carbonate to 100 ml of distilled water. Heat to $80°C$ and add 10.0 mg of bilirubin.)
2. Swinex filter the above and dispense into sterile screw cap tubes. Shelf-life is six months at $5°C$. Freeze the remainder.

Range of Expected Reaction:

pH	Protein	Glucose	Ketones	Bilirubin	Blood	Urobilinogen	Specific Gravity
8.0	+ − ++	+ − ++	++	+	++	1	1.006
							1.010

SUGGESTIONS

1. Store the dipsticks according to the manufacturer's specifications.
2. If a refractometer or urinometer is used to determine specific gravity, the refractometer should be calibrated each day of use with both distilled water and the control. Record the results.
3. Run the control at the beginning of each day and with each batch of tests.
4. Run every tenth specimen in duplicate as a precision check.

SPECIMEN CONDITION

If the specimens cannot be run immediately, refrigerate them. Specimens should be run no later than four hours after collection even though they have been refrigerated.

chapter twelve Remedial Action

A LOGICAL SEQUENCE OF EVENTS

The procedures in Chapters 1 through 11 help to ensure the accuracy and precision of reported results, but they will not totally eliminate errors. The techniques, if applied properly, should restrict the errors to a minimum, ensure that the laboratory provides reliable data, and bring subtle deviations from expected results to the attention of the analyst.

If the quality control techniques are to be properly used to accomplish the above, then the techniques must be monitored at regular intervals by the analyst, the supervisor, and the director. The authors' laboratory uses several techniques for monitoring quality control data and taking remedial action.

The regulatory aspects of quality control can be portrayed in much the same manner as a computer program analyst sets up a solution to a problem by first making a flow chart of the solution (Figure 8).

Notice that, once the process of quality control is begun, there is no way out of the loop. This is intentional because quality control in a clinical setting is a continuing process. The process only stops when the laboratory ceases operation.

Internal quality control results should be monitored daily by the analyst and the immediate supervisor, weekly by the division director or chief technologist and quality control officer (if there is one), and monthly by the laboratory director. In addition, results of external quality control (proficiency testing) analysis should be routed to each individual concerned with the analysis.

The laboratory procedures manuals should be continuously reviewed and kept current by the supervisor, and it should be annually reviewed and signed by both the supervisor and the laboratory director.

Each discipline should maintain a section in the quality control records for recording out-of-control results, problems with media, reagents, chemicals, and the action taken to correct the situation. A complete description of the source of the problem and the steps taken to prevent a recurrence also should be recorded.

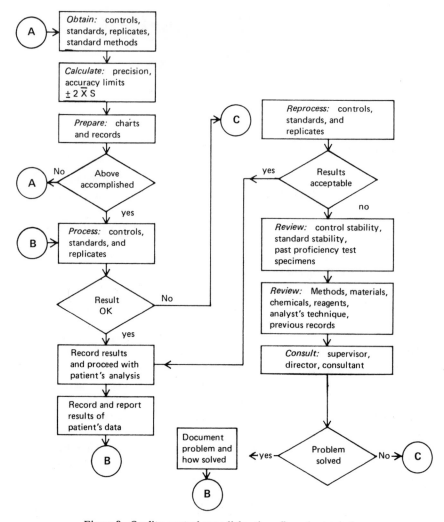

Figure 8. Quality control remedial action: flow chart solution.

EXAMPLES OF PROBLEMS AND ACTIONS TAKEN

Example 1

Zone sizes for antibiotic sensitivity discs would not fall into the acceptable ranges specified by NCCLS (refer to Table 11) using the three control organisms.

1. Controls were repeated, but results continued to be unacceptable.
2. Discs were found to be adequate, i.e., expiration dates and conditions of storage were being observed.
3. The pH of the Mueller-Hinton agar was within acceptable limits, and gross observation of the agar revealed a small amount of precipitate.
4. The McFarland Standard (several months old) became suspect, as did the medium.
5. New standard was prepared and medium was obtained from another source.
6. The test was repeated with old versus new standard and new medium.
7. In both instances, the zone sizes fell within acceptable limits, leading us to believe that the medium was somehow deficient.
8. The analyst wrote, "while the pH of the medium appeared to be in order, the medium date of preparation was listed at 4½ weeks from the time of the test problem." Check-testing before use had not been performed.
9. Corrective action:
   "Mueller-Hinton medium will be prepared weekly and stored at 5°C with dessicant. The medium will be checked for reliability each week and whenever a test is performed."

Example 2

Brain heart infusion agar was used to transplant a test organism (*Dermatophilus congolensis*) used in a research project. The organism was obtained in a viable state from the Center for Disease Control, but could not be grown on the brain heart slants in our laboratory. Other media prepared in-house supported the growth of this organism.

1. The mycology section had just begun a quality control program and had not begun testing the ability of certain types of media to perform.
2. Brain heart infusion agar obviously became suspect; therefore, it was decided that *Staphylococcus aureus* would be used to test the ability of the brain heart slants to support growth.
3. The media supervisor was brought in for consultation, and, during the course of the conversation, it became evident that media preparation was placing penicillin in the agar. This was a procedure set up in the past for inhibiting bacteria while allowing certain fungi and yeast to flourish. The section had never been instructed to discontinue the addition of penicillin to the brain heart infusion agar slants.

Example 3

The clinical chemistry section was testing a new lot of controls against the previous lot before its use. The new lot repeatedly fell well below the "acceptable range" as specified in the package insert. The "old lot" performed satisfactorily.

1. The control serum was found to be defective. The manufacturer replaced the lot without question.

One could continue with examples of control problems and failures ad infinitum; however, the point must be obvious. The standards and control measures ensure a reasonable level of accuracy and precision if used properly. They facilitate the ability of the analyst to pinpoint problem areas before a major problem occurs.

It is mandatory for each section in the laboratory to maintain a record entitled "Remedial Action." This record should contain the date of the problem, a complete description of the problem, the steps taken to alleviate the problem, and the signatures of the analyst and chief technologist.

REMEDIAL ACTION IN RETROSPECT

A review of quality control records in all disciplines in the laboratory for the past three years revealed several important points:

1. Routine, standardized procedures seldom require remedial action. When they do, the problem is usually with a new lot of reagents or a new batch of media.
2. Relatively new and untried procedures show a very high failure rate at the outset. The reasons frequently are attributed to the inexperience of the analyst with the procedure and with the equipment and not with deteriorated controls, reagents, or standards.
3. A rigorous quality control program in media and reagent preparation decreases quality control failures, complaints, and reprocessing of specimens in the sections.
4. *Major* analytical errors all but disappear, and subtle variations are detected and corrected before they become major problems.

RECOURSE TO
DEFECTIVE LABORATORY SUPPLIES AND EQUIPMENT

The Medical Device and Laboratory Product Problem Reporting Program was initiated in 1973 for the purpose of improving product quality and informing both the government and manufacturer of health hazards.

The program is coordinated by the United States Pharmacopeia (USP) and draws on the expertise of some 300 representatives from colleges of pharmacy and medicine.

The program urges the user to report anything considered to be a problem. This may involve improper labeling, defective components, performance failures, poor packaging, incomplete or confusing instructions, erroneous information, improvements, and health hazards. USP's motto: "When in doubt, report."

A simple, one-page form, the Medical Device and Laboratory Product Report Form #2519, is available to make reporting easy. It may be obtained by writing to: United States Pharmacopeia, 12601 Twinbrook Parkway, Rockville, Maryland 20852.

The reporting program works as follows:

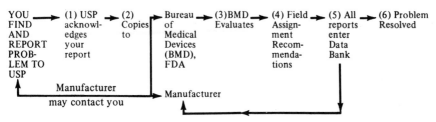

Without your input, manufacturers, government, and the rest of the health care community may not be aware of the problems you experience.

appendix An Interim Laboratory Checklist

The following checklist was prepared by the Center for Disease Control Licensure and Proficiency Testing Division and is reproduced with written permission of the Examination and Documentation Branch.

The reader should be advised that certain items on this checklist may be revised in 1977.

The checklist covers every aspect of a clinical laboratory requiring certification. It also gives the number of the appropriate federal regulation which requires compliance with each item.

The authors suggest that this checklist be used while reading and implementing the practices suggested in this text. The checklist covers material not found in the text and therefore provides a very useful supplement.

DIRECTIONS FOR COMPLETING INTERIM CHECKLIST

The checklist has been designed to standardize the survey process, provide specific questions which are supported by the regulations, and to minimize the necessity for narrative answers. Each question requires a response in one of three columns: "Yes," "No," or "Not Applicable." Any "No" response is considered a deficiency. Where appropriate, space is provided to document or identify the specific deficiency such as equipment, test, procedure, reagent, etc.

The checklist is divided into two major sections—Laboratory Management and Quality Control.

The first section, Laboratory Management, deals with conditions for coverage in sections 405.1311 through 405.1316 of the Medicare regulations. Questions in this part are considered self-explanatory.

The second section, Laboratory Quality Control, deals with conditions for coverage in section 405.1317. This section contains an individual checklist for each of the following eighteen categories/subcategories:

Bacteriology (p. 121)   Immunohematology (p. 180)
Mycology (p. 128)   Hematology (p. 187)

Parasitology (p. 133)   Cytology (p. 194)
Virology (p. 138)   Histology (p. 194)
Syphilis Serology (p. 148)   Radiobioassay (p. 204)
Non-Syphilis Serology (p. 156) Histocompatibility (p. 208)
Clinical Chemistry (p. 162)   Blood and Cerebrospinal Fluid Chemistry
Cytogenetics (p. 170)   Endocrinology
Urinalysis (p. 175)   Toxicology

The page numbers given in parentheses after each category/subcategory indicate the page on which that checklist begins. Those categories with no accompanying page numbers are not reproduced in this Appendix.

A "Floater" sheet (not included in this Appendix) also has been designed to be used in each subcategory. It consists of 33 general questions, applicable to each of the 15 subcategories, which correlate with the questions on the checklists. There is space provided for documentation of preventive maintenance and procedural manual deficiencies. Each of the 33 questions on the floater sheet is to be marked and documented in the appropriate subcategory.

DEPARTMENT OF HEALTH, EDUCATION, & WELFARE CENTER FOR
DISEASE CONTROL
Bureau of Laboratories, Licensure and Proficiency Testing
Field Examination Section Checklist and Report

Laboratory Code CLIA _____

Provider No. SSA _____

2. Laboratory Name	3. Date

4. Name of Examiner(s)/Surveyor(s)

5. Address and Zip Code of Laboratory
(Telephone   )

7. Director

6. Examination Time Spent at Clinical Laboratory
Arrival Time: _____   Departure Time: _____

8. Technical Supervisor

9. Type of Exam
Original / / / Annual / / / Reexamination / / / Follow Up / / / Other
Medicare / / /   / / /   / / /   / / /
State   / / /   / / /   / / /   / / /
CLIA   / / /   / / /   / / /   / / /

10. CATEGORIES	LICENSED	CERTIFIED	EXAMINED	WORKLOAD
Bacteriology (110)	____	____	____	____
Mycology (120)	____	____	____	____
Parasitology (130)	____	____	____	____
Virology (140)	____	____	____	____
Other (150)	____	____	____	____
Syphilis Serology (210)	____	____	____	____
General Serology (220)	____	____	____	____
Routine Chemistry (310)	____	____	____	____
Endocrinology (330)	____	____	____	____
Toxicology (330)	____	____	____	____
Urinalysis (320)	____	____	____	____

continued

Immunohematology (500) _____
Hematology (400) _____
Cytology (630) _____
Histopathology (610) _____
Oral Pathology (620) _____
Radiobioassay (800) _____
Histocompatibility (950) _____
Other _____

Supervisors _____

HOURS OF OPERATION:

	Shift 1	Shift 2	Shift 3
M.	_____	_____	_____
T.	_____	_____	_____
W.	_____	_____	_____
T.	_____	_____	_____
F.	_____	_____	_____
S.	_____	_____	_____
S.	_____	_____	_____

11. Overall On-site Examination Discussed With:

Examiner(s) _____

Surveyor(s) _____

	CFR No.	Yes	No	NA	Comments–Identify by Number

LABORATORY MANAGEMENT

STATE OR LOCAL LICENSING

1. If the laboratory is located in a state which has a
E7   state or local law licensing laboratories and
E9   personnel, the laboratory is:

    a. Licensed in accordance with applicable laws.   405.1311(a)
      Current permit date _____.

E11   b. The director is licensed or registered.   405.1311(b)

E11   c. Each technical staff member is licensed or   405.1311(b)
      registered.

E13   d. Laboratory is in accordance with applicable   405.1311(c)
      fire, safety and other relevant laws.

DIRECTOR

2. The clinical laboratory is under the direction of a   405.1312
E16   qualified person.

3. The director serves the laboratory on a full-time   405.1312(a)
E18   or regular part-time basis.   (1)

4. The director individually serves no more than   405.1312(a)
E18   three (3) institutions unless a qualified associate   (1)(i)(ii)
    director is provided in each additional
    laboratory.

5. Commensurate with the laboratory workload the

continued

111

Laboratory Code _____

	CFR No.	Yes	No	NA	Comments—Identify by Number

LABORATORY MANAGEMENT—*Continued*

DIRECTOR—*Continued*

	CFR No.	Yes	No	NA	Comments
E21 director spends an adequate amount of time in the laboratory. No. hrs. spent in laboratory ____/week.(2)	405.1312(a)				
E9					
6. If continuously absent for more than one month E33 a qualified substitute is provided. Name of substitute ____.	405.1312(a)(5)				

SUPERVISORS

	CFR No.	Yes	No	NA	Comments
7. The technical supervisor spends an adequate E42 amount of time in the laboratory and is available for consultation. No. hrs. in laboratory ____/week.	405.1313(a)(1)				
8. The laboratory has a general supervisor on the E39 premises during all hours testing is performed.	405.1313(a)(1)				
9. All work performed as an "Emergency" outside E43 regularly scheduled duty hours is reviewed the following duty period by a supervisor	405.1313(a)(2)				
10. The laboratory performs only those laboratory E70 procedures that are within the specialties or subspecialties in which the laboratory director or supervisors are qualified.	405.1314(b)				

112

TECHNICAL PERSONNEL

11. The clinical laboratory has a sufficient number			
E107 of properly qualified technical personnel for the volume and diversity of tests performed.	405.1315		
12. A. Technologists:			
E108 1. The laboratory employs a sufficient number of clinical laboratory technologists to proficiently perform under general supervision the clinical laboratory tests which require the exercise of independent judgment.	405.1315(a)		
E111 2. The technologists perform the tests requiring the exercise of independent judgment and responsibility with minimal supervision only in specialties qualified.	405.1315(1)		
E112 3. Specialties in which the technologist is not qualified are performed only under direct supervision.	405.1315(2)		
E113 4. Technologists are in sufficient number to supervise the work of technicians and trainees.	405.1315(3)		
13. B. Cytotechnologists			
E108 1. The laboratory employs a sufficient number of cytotechnologists to proficiently perform under general supervision the laboratory tests which require the exercise of independent judgment.	405.1315(a)		

continued

113

	CFR No.	Yes	No	NA	Comments–Identify by Number
LABORATORY MANAGEMENT–*Continued*					
TECHNICAL PERSONNEL–*Continued*					
E114 2. Cytotechnologists supervise technicians and trainees only in the specialty of cytology.	405.1315(4)				
14. C. Technicians					
E121 1. Technicians are employed in sufficient number to meet the workload demands of the laboratory and function only under direct supervision.	405.1315(d)				
E122 2. Technicians perform only procedures which require a degree of skill commensurate with education, training and involve limited exercise of independent judgment.	405.1315(1)				
E123 3. No technician performs procedures in the absence of a qualified technologist, supervisor, or director.	405.1315(2)				
15. D. Trainee					
E124 A technician trainee performs only repetitive procedures which require a minimal exercise of independent judgment, and may perform such procedures only under the personal and direct supervision of a qualified supervisor or technologist.	405.1315(3)				

PERSONNEL POLICIES

	Reference				
16. The laboratory maintains written personnel polices and current personnel records for each employee.	74.52 405.1315(f)				
E129 Personnel records contain the following: a. training	.52 .1315(f)				
E129 b. experience	.52 .1315(f)				
E129 c. duties	.52 .1315(f)				
E129 d. dates of employment	.52 .1315(f)				
E130 e. evidence of adequate health supervision	.1315(f)				
E130 f. reports of illnesses and accident occurring on duty	.52 .1315(f)				

PHYSICAL FACILITIES AND SAFETY

	Reference				
17. Workbench space is: E137 a. ample	74.20(b) 74.55 405.1316(b)(1)				
E137 b. well lighted	.20(b) .55 .1316(b)(1)				
E137 c. convenient to all necessary facilities	.20(b) .55 .1316(b)(1)				

continued

LABORATORY MANAGEMENT—*Continued*

PHYSICAL FACILITIES AND SAFETY—*Continued*

		CFR No.	Yes	No	NA	Comments—Identify by Number
18.	Work areas are arranged to minimize problems in:					
E138	a. transportation	.20(b) .55 .1316(b)(2)				
E138	b. communication	.20(b) .55 .1316(b)(2)				
E138	c. ventilation	.20(b) .55 .1316(b)(3)				
19. E142	Adequate fire precautions and occupational safety and health laws are known, posted, and observed.	.1316(b)(7)				
20. E140	The laboratory is free of unnecessary hazards:	.1316(b)(7)				
E140	a. physical	.1316(b)(7)				
E140	b. chemical	.1316(b)(7)				
E140	c. biological	.1316(b)(7)				

SPECIMEN COLLECTION

		CFR No.	Yes	No	NA	Comments—Identify by Number
21. E143	Only a licensed physician, or one otherwise authorized by law, collects specimens.	405.1316(c)				
22. E143	Qualified technical personnel collect specimens under the direction or upon the written request of a licensed physician.	405.1316(c)				

116

STERILIZATION

23. E145	Blood-letting devices (syringes, needles, lancets, etc.) are:			
E145	a. disposable or, if not, properly sterilized prior to each use.	405.1316(d)		
E145	b. wrapped in a manner to ensure sterility until use.	405.1316(d)		
E145	c. disposable appropriately discarded after use.	405.1316(d)		
24. E146	Appropriate techniques are utilized for tests performed on potentially contaminated material.	405.1316(d)		
25. E148	Each sterilizing cycle contains: a. a device which indicates proper sterilization or an adequate recording thermometer is used.	74.20(b) 405.1316(d)		
E148	b. records document results if recording thermometer is used.	.1316(d)		
E149	c. the autoclave is checked monthly with viable spores.	74.20(b) 405.1316(d)		
E132	d. records document results of spore checks.	74.20(f) 405.1316(d)		

EXAMINATION AND REPORTS

26. E150	The laboratory examines specimens only at the request of a licensed physician, dentist, or other person authorized by law to use the findings of the laboratory examinations.	405.1316(e)		

continued

Laboratory Code

	CFR No.	Yes	No	NA	Comments—Identify by Number
LABORATORY MANAGEMENT—*Continued*					
EXAMINATION AND REPORTS—*Continued*					
27. If a patient is sent to the laboratory, a written E151 request for the desired procedure is obtained.	405.1316(e)				
28. Each specimen received in the laboratory is E152 accompanied by a written request.	405.1316(e)				
29. If the laboratory receives specimens from E153 another laboratory, it reports back to the laboratory submitting the specimens.	405.1316(e)				
SPECIMENS-RECORDS ACCESSION					
30. Daily accession records on specimens are E154 maintained and contain:	74.53 405.1316(f)				
E155 a. laboratory number or other identification.	.53 .1316(f)				
E156 b. name or identification of person from which specimen was taken.	.53 .1316(f)				
E157 c. name or identification of person who submitted specimen.	.53 .1316(f)				
E158 d. date specimen was collected.	.53 .1316(f)				
E159 e. date specimen received in laboratory.	.53 .1316(f)				
E161 f. type of test performed.	.53 .1316(f)				

118

continued

E162	g.	date test performed.	.53 .1316(f)			
E163	h.	results of test, or cross-reference to results.	.53 .1316(f)			
E163	i.	date of reporting.	.53 .1316(f)			
E160	j.	condition of unsatisfactory specimens when received.	.53 .1316(f)			
E164	k.	name and address of laboratory to which specimen is forwarded if the procedure is not performed at this laboratory.	.53 .1316(f)			

LABORATORY RECORDS AND REPORTS

	31.	The laboratory report is sent promptly to authorized person requesting the test.	74.54(a) 405.1316(b)			
E167	32.	Duplicate copies or a suitable record of laboratory reports are filed in laboratory in a manner which permits ready identification and accessibility.	405.1316(g)			
E165	33.	Suitable records of all test results are preserved by the laboratory for a period of at least 2 years after the date of submittal of the report or for a period of time required by state law for such records, whichever is longer.	74.54(a) 405.1316(g)			
E166	34.	The laboratory director is responsible for the report.	405.1316(g)(1)			
	35.	If the specimen is referred to another laboratory,				

119

Laboratory Code

	CFR No.	Yes	No	NA	Comments—Identify by Number
LABORATORY MANAGEMENT—*Continued*					
LABORATORY RECORDS AND REPORTS—*Continued*					
E172 the laboratory receiving the specimen meets the conditions under the health insurance program.	405.1316(g)(7)				
36. E173 Each authorized person requesting an examination is notified that the specimen was referred to another laboratory.	405.1316(g)(7)				
37. E174 The name and address of the laboratory actually performing the examination are indicated in the report to the person submitting the specimen.	74.54(a) 405.1316(g)(7)				
38. E169 The results of a laboratory test, procedure, or transcript is given to the patient concerned only with the written consent of the authorized person requesting the test.	405.1316(g)(4)				
39. E170 Pertinent "normal" ranges as determined by the laboratory performing the tests are available to the authorized person requesting such tests.	74.54(d) 405.1316(g)(5)				
40. E171 A list of analytical methods employed by the laboratory and a basis for the listed "normal" range is maintained in the laboratory.	405.1316(g)(6)				
41. E171 A list of analytical methods employed by the laboratory is available to any authorized person ordering an examination.	74.54(d) 405.1316(g)(6)				

	CFR No.	Yes	No	NA	Comments–Identify by Number

BACTERIOLOGY 74.21(a)-405.1317(b)(1)

PREVENTIVE MAINTENANCE 74.20(a)-405.1317(a)(1)

		CFR No.	Yes	No	NA	Comments–Identify by Number
E177	1. There is a preventive maintenance program for each piece of equipment.	74.20(a) 405.1317(a)(1)				
E132	2. Records are available to document that a preventive maintenance program is in operation and include:	74.20(f) 405.1316				
E132	a. Instrument name	.20(f) .1316				
E132	b. Date installed (if available)	74.20(f) .1316				
E132	c. Serial number	.20(f) .1316				
E132	d. Number to call for service	.20(f) .1316				
E132	e. Date of service	.20(f) .1316				
E132	f. Nature of service	.20(f) .1316				
E132	g. Initials of person servicing	.20(f) .1316				
E132	h. Date of next service or service schedule	.20(f) .1316				

continued

121

BACTERIOLOGY 74.21(a)-405.1317(b)(1)—*Continued*

PREVENTIVE MAINTENANCE 74.20(a)-405.1317(a)(1)—*Continued*

	CFR No.	Yes	No	NA	Comments—Identify by Number
E132 i. Results recorded	74.50				
2. All remedial actions are taken to correct					
E180 detected defects before patient results are reported. Recorded: Yes ___ No ___	74.20(b) 405.1317(a)(1)				

TEMPERATURES

	CFR No.	Yes	No	NA	Comments—Identify by Number
3. The following temperature controlled spaces and					
E187 equipment are monitored each day: a. Incubators	74.20(a) 405.1371(a)(2)				
E187 b. Refrigerators	74.20(b) .1317(a)(2)				
E187 c. Waterbaths	.20(b) .1317(a)(2)				
E187 d. Heatblocks	.20(b) .1317(a)(2)				
E187 e. Freezers	.20(b) .1317(a)(2)				
E187 f. Ambient (when critical to test)	.20(b) .1317(a)(2)				
E132 g. Recorded	74.50 405.1316				

122

STANDARD OPERATING PROCEDURE MANUAL

E193	A complete written description of methods in use is in the immediate bench area where personnel are engaged in examining specimens:	74.20(d) 405.1317(a)(4)	
	SOPM includes:		
E194	a. Methods in use	.20(d) .1317(a)(4)	
E196	b. Control procedures	.20(a) .1317(a)(4)	
E195	c. Reagents	.20(a) .1317(a)(4)	
E197	d. Literature references	.20(d) .1317(a)(4)	
E134	e. An annual review and date by the technical supervisor	.20(e) .1316(a)	
E198	f. All changes initialed and dated by the technical supervisor	.1317(a)(5)	
E197	g. Textbooks are used as supplements only	74.20(d) .1317(a)(4)	

REAGENTS

5.	Reagent labels include:	74.20(c) 405.1317(a)(3)	
E188	a. Identity (name, lot number)		
E191	b. A date (prepared, received, opened or expiration)	.20(c) .1517(a)(3)	
E189	c. Concentration, titer, or strength	.20(c) .1517(a)(3)	

continued

Laboratory Code

BACTERIOLOGY 74.21(a)-405.1317(b)(1)—*Continued*

REAGENTS—*Continued*

Code	Item	CFR No.	Yes	No	NA	Comments–Identify by Number
E190	d. Recommended storage (if pertinent)	.20(c) .1517(a)(3)				
	6. All chemical and biological solutions and					
E211	reagents are tested each day of use with selective organism to ensure:					
E211	a. Positive biochemical reaction	74.21(a) 405.1317(b)(1)				
E211	b. Negative biochemical reaction	.21(a) .1317(b)(1)				
E132	c. Results recorded	74.50 405.1316				
	7. Selective organisms are used each new vial and					
E211	weekly to check:	**				
	a. Positive biochemical reaction of discs					
E211	b. Negative biochemical reaction of discs	**				
E211	c. Positive biochemical reaction of strips	**				
E211	d. Negative biochemical reaction of strips	**				
E132	e. Results recorded	74.50 405.1316				
	8. Antisera is checked each new vial and each month					
E217	of use with selective organisms to ensure:	**				
	a. Positive agglutination					
E217	b. Negative agglutination	**				

124

E132	c. Results recorded	74.50 / 405.1316		
9. E192	The laboratory does not use deteriorated materials or materials of substandard reactivity.	74.20 / 405.1317(a)(3)		

STAINS

10. E213	All stains (except Gram) are tested each day of use with organisms to produce predicted staining characteristics.	74.21(a) / 405.1317(b)(1)		
11. E213	Gram stain is checked each new batch and once per week with selected organisms to produce: a. Gram positive reactions	**		
E213	b. Gram negative reactions	**		
E132	c. Results of stain checks recorded	74.50 / 405.1316		

MEDIA

12. E214	Each batch of media is tested to confirm: a. Growth characteristics	74.21(a) / 405.1317(a)(1)		
E214	b. Selectivity	.21(a) / .1317(b)(1)		
E214	c. Enrichment	.21(a) / .1317(b)(3)		
E214	d. Biochemical response	.21(a) / .1317(b)(1)		
E132	f. Results recorded	74.50 / 405.1316		

continued

	CFR No.	Yes	No	NA	Comments–Identify by Number
BACTERIOLOGY 74.21(a)-405.1317(b)(1)–*Continued*					
SUSCEPTIBILITY TESTING					
13. With Kirby-Bauer or Agar Overlay methods, discs are checked each day of use with:					
E218 a. *Escherichia coli* (ATCC)	74.21 405.1317(b)(1)				
E218 b. *Staphylococcus aureus* (ATCC)	.21(a) .1317(b)(1)				
E132 c. Zone size recorded	74.50 405.1316				
14. With methods other than Kirby-Bauer or Agar Overlay, discs are checked each week of use with:					
E218 a. *Escherichia coli* (ATCC)	74.21(a) 405.1317( )(6)				
E218 b. *Staphylococcus aureus* (ATCC)	.21(a) .1317(b)(1)				
E132 c. Zone size recorded	74.50 405.1316				
15. With automated susceptibility testing each day of use:					
E218 a. *Escherichia coli* (ATCC) is checked	74.21(a) 405.1317(b)(1)				
E218 b. *Staphylococcus aureus* (ATCC) is checked	.21(a) .1317(b)(1)				
E218 c. Instrument is calibrated with filter	74.20 .1317(a)(2)				
E132 d. Results recorded	74.50 405.1316				

MYCOBACTERIOLOGY

16. Each batch of media is checked with an acid fast organism for:			
E214 a. Growth requirements	74.21(a) 405.1317(b)( )		
E132 b. Results recorded	74.50 405.1316		
17. Reagents used in the identification of AFB are checked each day of use to ensure:			
E211 a. Positive response	74.21(a) 405.1317(b)(1)		
E211 b. Negative response	.21(a) .1317(b)(1)		
E132 c. Results recorded	74.50 405.1316		
18. Stains used for acid fast organisms are checked each day of use with:			
E213 a. Positive acid fast organism	74.21(a) 405.1317(b)(1)		
E132 b. Results recorded	74.50 405.1316		

RECORDS

19. Records document the results of each step taken			
E132 to obtain the patient result.	74.50 405.1316		
20. Daily accession assures proper identification of			
E154 specimens throughout the testing.	74.53 405.1316(f)		
21. All records retained at least 2 years.			
E165	74.54(a) 405.1316(g)		

**Administrative modification of daily requirement until regulations are revised.

	CFR No.	Yes	No	NA	Comments–Identify by Number

MYCOLOGY 74.21(a)–405.1317(b)(1)

PREVENTIVE MAINTENANCE 74.20(a)-405.1317(a)(1)

		CFR No.	Yes	No	NA	Comments–Identify by Number
E177	1. There is a preventive maintenance program for each piece of equipment.	74.20(a) 405.1317(a)(1)				
E132	2. Records are available to document that a preventive maintenance program is in operation and include: .1316	.50 .20(f) .1316				
E132	a. Instrument name	.20(f) .1316				
E132	b. Date installed (if available)	74.20(f) .1316				
E132	c. Serial number	.20(f) .1316				
E132	d. Number to call for service	.20(f) .1316				
E132	e. Date of service	.20(f) .1316				
E132	f. Nature of service	.20(f) .1316				
E132	g. Initials of person servicing	.20(f) .1316				

128

Code	Item	Reference		
E132	h. Date of next service or service schedule	.20(f) .1316		
E132	i. Results recorded	74.50 405.1316		
E180	2. All remedial actions are taken to correct detected defects before patient results are reported. Recorded: Yes___ No___	.50 .20(f) .1317(a)(1)		

TEMPERATURES 74.20(b)-405.1317(a)(2)

Code	Item	Reference					
E187	3. The following temperature-controlled spaces and equipment are monitored each day of use to ensure proper performance.	.20(b) .1317(a)(2)					
E187	a. Incubators	.20(b) .1317(a)(2)					
E187	b. Refrigerators	.20(b) .1317(a)(2)					
E187	c. Water baths	.20(b) .1317(a)(2)					
E187	d. Heat blocks	.20(b) .1317(a)(2)					
E187	e. Freezers	.20(b) .1317(a)(2)					
E187	f. Ambient (when critical to test)	.20(b) .1317(a)(2)					
E187	g. Recorded	74.50 405.1316					

continued

MYCOLOGY 74.21(a)–405.1317(b)(1)–*Continued*

STANDARD OPERATING PROCEDURE
MANUAL 74.20(d)–405.1317(a)(4)

	CFR No.	Yes	No	NA	Comments–Identify by Number
4. A complete written description of methods in E193 use is in the immediate bench area where personnel are engaged in examining specimens and includes:	74.20(d) 405.1317(a)(4)				
E194 a. Methods in use	.20(d) .1317(a)(4)				
E196 b. Control procedures	.20(d) .1317(a)(4)				
E195 c. Reagents	.20(d) .1317(a)(4)				
E197 d. Literature references	.20(d) .1317(a)(4)				
E134 e. An annual review and date by the technical supervisor	.20(e) .1316(a)				
E198 f. All changes initialed and dated by the technical supervisor	.1317(a)(5)				
E197 g. Textbooks are used as supplements only	74.20(d) .1317(a)(4)				

continued

REAGENTS 74.20(c)-405.1517(a)(3)

5. All reagents are properly labeled:			
E188 a. Identity (name, lot number)		.20(c) .1517(a)(3)	
E191 b. A date (prepared, received, opened, or expiration)		.20(c) .1517(a)(3)	
E189 c. Concentration, titer, or strength		.20(c) .1517(a)(3)	
E190 d. Recommended storage requirements (if pertinent)		.20(c) .1517(a)(3)	
6. The laboratory does not use materials of		.20(c)	
E192 substandard reactivity or deteriorated material.		.1517(a)(3)	
7. All chemical and biological solutions and			

E211   reagents are tested each day of use with selective
       organisms to ensure:
       a. Positive biochemical reactivity
		74.21(a)
		405.1317(b)(1)	

E211 b. Negative biochemical reactivity		.21(a) .1317(b)(1)	
E132 c. Results recorded		74.50 405.1316	

MEDIA 74.21(a)-405.1317(b)(1)

8. Each new batch of media is checked with known			
E214 organisms to confirm: a. Intended selectivity		74.21(a) 405.1317(b)(1)	
E214 b. Enrichment		.21(a) .1317(b)(1)	

MYCOLOGY 74.21(a)–405.1317(b)(1)—*Continued*

MEDIA 74.21(a)–405.1317(b)(1)—*Continued*

		CFR No.	Yes	No	NA	Comments–Identify by Number
E214	c. Biochemical response	.21(a) .1317(b)(1)				
E132	d. Results recorded	74.50 405.1316				

STAINS

		CFR No.	Yes	No	NA	Comments–Identify by Number
E213	9. All stains are tested each day of use with organisms to produce predicted staining characteristics.	74.21(a) 405.1317(b)(10)				
E132	a. Results of stain checks recorded.	74.50 405.1316				

RECORDS

		CFR No.	Yes	No	NA	Comments–Identify by Number
E132	10. a. Records document the results of each step taken to obtain the patient result.	74.50 405.1316				
E154	b. Daily accession assures proper identification of specimens throughout testing.	74.53 405.1316(f)				
E165	c. All records retained at least 2 years.	74.54(a) 405.1316(g)				

PARASITOLOGY 74.21(b)-405.1317(b)(ii)

PREVENTIVE MAINTENANCE 74.20(a)-405.1317(a)(1)

	CFR No.	Yes	No	NA	Comments – Identify by Number
E177 1. There is a preventive maintenance program for each piece of equipment.	74.20(a) 405.1317(a)(1)				
Records are available to document that a preventive maintenance program is in operation and include:	.50 .20(f) .1316				
E132 a. Instrument name	.20(f) .1316				
E132 b. Date installed (if available)	74.20(f) .1316				
E132 c. Serial number	.20(f) .1316				
E132 d. Number to call for service	.20(f) .1316				
E132 e. Date of service	.20(f) .1316				
E132 f. Nature of service	.20(f) .1316				
E132 g. Initials of person servicing	.20(f) .1316				

continued

133

	CFR No.	Yes	No	NA	Comments–Identify by Number

PARASITOLOGY 74.21(b)-
405.1317(b)(ii)–Continued

PREVENTIVE MAINTENANCE 74.20(a)-
405.1317(a)(1)–Continued

	CFR No.	Yes	No	NA	Comments–Identify by Number
E132 h. Date of next service or service schedule	.20(f) .1316				
E132 i. Results recorded	74.50 405.1316				
2. All remedial actions are taken to correct detected defects before patient results are reported. Recorded: Yes ___ No ___	.50 .20(f) .1317(a)(1)				

TEMPERATURES 74.20(b)-405.1317(a)(2)

	CFR No.	Yes	No	NA	Comments–Identify by Number
3. The following temperature-controlled spaces and equipment are monitored each day of use to assure proper performance.					
E187 a. Incubators	.20(b) .1317(a)(2)				
E187 b. Refrigerators	.20(b) .1317(a)(2)				
E187 c. Water baths	.20(b) .1317(a)(2)				
E187 d. Heat blocks	.20(b) .1317(a)(2)				
E187 e. Freezers	.20(b) .1317(a)(2)				

134

No.	Item	Reference			
E187	f. Ambient (when critical to test)	.20(b) .1317(a)(2)			
E132	g. Recorded	74.50 405.1316			

REAGENTS 74.20(c)-405.1517(a)(3)

No.	Item	Reference			
	4. All reagents are properly labeled:				
E188	a. Identity (name, lot number)	.20(c) .1517(a)(3)			
E191	b. A date (prepared, received, opened, or expiration)	.20(c) .1517(a)(3)			
E189	c. Concentration, titer, or strength	.20(c) .1517(a)(3)			
E190	d. Recommended storage requirements (if pertinent)	.20(c) .1517(a)(3)			
	5. The laboratory does not use materials of				
E192	substandard reactivity or deteriorated material	.20(c) .1517(a)(3)			

STANDARD OPERATING PROCEDURE MANUAL 74.20(d)-405.1317(a)(4)

No.	Item	Reference			
	6. A complete written description of methods in				
E193	use is in the immediate bench area where personnel are engaged in examining specimens.	.20(c) .1317(a)(4)			
E194	SOPM includes: a. Analytical methods in use	.20(d) .1317(a)(4)			
E196	b. Control procedures	.20(d) .1317(a)(4)			

continued

PARASITOLOGY 74.21(b)-405.1317(b)(ii)–*Continued*

STANDARD OPERATING PROCEDURE
MANUAL 74.20(d)-405.1317(a)(4)–*Continued*

	CFR No.	Yes	No	NA	Comments–Identify by Number
E196 c. Calibration procedures	.20(d) .1317(a)(4)				
E195 d. Reagents	.20(d) .1317(a)(4)				
E197 e. Pertinent literature references	.20(d) .1317(a)(4)				
E134 f. Annual review and date by technical supervisor	.20(e) .1316(a)				
E198 g. Changes initialed and dated by technical supervisor	.1317(a)(5)				

QUALITY CONTROL 74.21(b)-405.1317(b)(ii)

	CFR No.	Yes	No	NA	Comments–Identify by Number
7. The laboratory has a reference collection of at least one of the following: slides, photographs, or gross specimens.					
E220	.21(b) .1317(b)(1)				
8. The laboratory has an ocular micrometer that:					
E221 a. Has been calibrated by the laboratory	.21(b) .1317(b)(ii)				
E132 b. Records document calibration	.50 .1316				

9. Stains used for fecal specimens:			
E223 a. Are tested each new batch and once per month of use	74.21		
E132 b. Stain checks are recorded	.20(f) .1316(b)		
10. Reagents are inspected each day of use for E223 reactivity and deterioration	74.21 .1317(b)(1)		

RECORDS

11. a. Records document the results of each step E132 taken to obtain the patient result	74.50 405.1316		
E154 b. Daily accession assures proper identification of specimens throughout testing	74.53 405.1316(f)		
E165 c. All records retained at least 2 years	74.54(a) 405.1316(g)		

VIROLOGY 74.21(c)-405.1317(b)(1)(iii)

PREVENTIVE MAINTENANCE 74.20(a)-405.1317(a)(1)

		CFR No.	Yes	No	NA	Comments–Identify by Number
						Laboratory Code
E177	1. There is a preventive maintenance program for each piece of equipment.	74.20(a) 405.1317(a)(1)				
E132	Records are available to document that a preventive maintenance program is in operation and include:	.50 .20(f) .1316				
E132	a. Instrument name	.20(f) .1317(a)(1)				
E132	b. Date installed (if available)	.20(f) .1316				
E132	c. Serial number	.20(f) .1316				
E132	d. Number to call for service	.20(f) .1316				
E132	e. Date of service	.20(f) .1316				
E132	f. Nature of service	.20(f) .1316				
E132	g. Initials of person servicing	.20(f) .1316				
E132	h. Date of next service or service schedule	.20(f) .1316				

2. E180 All remedial actions are taken to correct detected defects before patient results are reported. Recorded: Yes ___ No ___	.50 .20(f) .1316	

TEMPERATURES 74.20(b)-405.1317(a)(2)

3. E187 The following temperature-controlled spaces and equipment are monitored each day of use to ensure proper performance.	.20(b) .1317(a)(2)	
E187 a. Incubators	.20(b) .1317(a)(2)	
E187 b. Refrigerators	.20(b) .1317(a)(2)	
E187 c. Water baths	.20(b) .1317(a)(2)	
E187 d. Heat blocks	.20(b) .1317(a)(2)	
E187 e. Freezers	.20(b) .1317(a)(2)	
E187 f. Ambient	.20(b) .1317(a)(2)	
E187 g. Recorded	74.50 405.1316	

REAGENTS 74.20(c)-405.1317(a)(3)

4. E188 Reagents are properly labeled: a. identity (name, lot number)	74.20(c) 405.1317(a)(3)	

continued

VIROLOGY 74.21(c)-405.1317(b)(1)(iii)—Continued

REAGENTS 74.20(c)-405.1317(a)(3)—Continued

	CFR No.	Yes	No	NA	Comments—Identify by Number
E191 b. a date (prepared, received, opened, or expiration)	.20(c) .1317(a)(3)				
E189 c. concentration, titer, or strength	.20(c) .1317(a)(3)				
E190 d. recommended storage requirements (if pertinent)	.20(c) .1317(a)(3)				
5. The laboratory does not use deteriorated E192 materials or materials of substandard reactivity.	74.20(c) 405.1317(a)(3)				
6. Each new lot of reagent is tested concurrently with one of known acceptable reactivity before the new reagent is placed in routine use.	74.22(b) 405.1317(b)(2)(ii)				
E132 Results recorded.	74.50 405.1316				

STANDARD OPERATING PROCEDURE MANUAL 74.20(d)-405.1317(a)(4)

	CFR No.	Yes	No	NA	Comments—Identify by Number
7. A complete written description of methods in E193 use is in the immediate bench area where personnel are engaged in examining specimens. SOPM includes:	.20(d) .1317(a)(4)				
E194 a. Analytical methods in use	.20(d) .1317(a)(4)				

continued

		Control procedures	.20(d) .1317(a)(4)			
E196	b.	Control procedures	.20(d) .1317(a)(4)			
E196	c.	Calibration procedures	.20(d) .1317(a)(4)			
E195	d.	Reagents	.20(d) .1317(a)(4)			
E197	e.	Pertinent literature references	.20(d) .1317(a)(4)			
E134	f.	Annual review and date by technical supervisor	.20(e) .1316(a)			
E198	g.	Changes initialed and dated by technical supervisor	.1317(a)(5)			
ISOLATION						
8.		The laboratory has systems for the isolation of	74.21(c)			
E225		viruses for which services are offered as follows:	405.1317(b)(1) (iii)			
ORTHOMYXOVIRUS						
E225	a.	Influenza A & B-primary monkey kidney cell culture and/or embryonated eggs.				
	b.	Influenza C-embryonated eggs.				
MYXOVIRUS-PARAMYXOVIRUS						
E225	a.	Parainfluenza-primary monkey kidney or established cell lines.				
	b.	Respiratory Syncytial Virus-RSV established cell lines.				

141

	CFR No.	Yes	No	NA	Comments—Identify by Number

VIROLOGY 74.21(c)-405.1317(b)(1)(iii)—*Continued*

ISOLATION—*Continued*

   c. Mumps-embryonated eggs or primary monkey or human kidney cells or established cell lines.

   d. Measles-primary monkey or human kidney or established cell lines.

E225   *REOVIRUS*—Primary monkey kidney or established cell lines.

E225   *PICORNAVIRUS*

   a. Polio and ECHO-primary or established cell lines.

   b. Coxsackie-primary or established cell lines and suckling mice.

E225   *HERPESVIRUS*

   a. Herpes simplex-embryonated eggs, primary or established cell lines, suckling mice, adult mice, or rabbits.

   b. Cytomegalovirus (CMV)-primary or established cell lines.

   c. Varicella (chicken pox) and Herpes zoster-embryonated eggs or established cell lines.

POX VIRUS—embryonated eggs *and* primary or established cell culture.

ADENOVIRUS–established or primary cell cultures.							
TOGAVIRUS-RUBELLA–primary Green monkey kidney cells culture or BHK-21 cell lines.							
RHINOVIRUS–human diploid cell lines or primary embryonic kidney.							
ARBOVIRUS–suckling mice or 1/2 day old chick, and established cell line.							
E226	a. Records are available which document the systems used for isolation.	74.21(c)					
E226	b. Reactions observed during isolation are recorded.	74.50 405.1316					
E227	c. Controls of uninoculated host systems are included with unknown specimens to identify erroneous results.	74.21(c) .1317(b)(1) (iii)					
E132	d. Records document control.	74.50 405.1316					

IDENTIFICATION

9. E225	The laboratory has reagents for the identification of viruses for which services are offered.	74.21(c) 405.1317(b)(1) (iii)		
10. E227	Each test on unknown specimens is run concurrently with: a. A positive or graded reactive serum control.	.21(c) .1317(b)(1) (iii)		
E227	b. Negative control.	.21(c) .1317(b)(1) (iii)		

continued

143

VIROLOGY 74.21(c)-405.1317(b)(1)(iii)—*Continued*

IDENTIFICATION—*Continued*

		CFR No.	Yes	No	NA	Comments—Identify by Number
E132	c. Results recorded.	.21(c) 405.1316				
E227	11. Controls for all test components are included as follows:	.21(c) .1317(b)(1) (iii)				
E227	a. Complement-Fixation tests 1. Hemolysin titrated with each new cell batch. 2. Complement titrated each time test performed. 3. Serum complement control included each time test performed. 4. Tissue antigen-complement control included each time test performed. 5. Antigen complement control included each time test performed. 6. Buffer-complement control included each time test performed. 7. Red cell control included each time test performed. 8. Results recorded.	74.50 405.1316				
E227	b. Hemagglutination-Inhibition tests	.21(c) .1317(b)(1) (iii)				

144

continued

E227	1. Antigen back titrated each time test performed. 2. Serum/cell/buffer control included each time test performed. 3. Cell/buffer control included each time test performed. 4. Results recorded.	74.50 405.1316	
E227	c. Neutralization tests	.21(c) .1317(b)(1) (iii)	
E227	1. TCD 50 determined each time test performed. 2. Normal serum/NS/antigen control included each time test performed. 3. Cell culture control included each time test performed. 4. Serum toxicity control included each time test performed. 5. Results recorded.	75.50 405.1316	
E227	d. Hemabsorption-Inhibition tests	.21(c) .1317(b)(1) (iii)	
E227	1. Cell culture control included each time test performed. 2. Results of cell culture control.	74.50 405.1316	

145

Laboratory Code

	CFR No.	Yes	No	NA	Comments—Identify by Number

VIROLOGY 74.21(c)-405.1317(b)(1)(iii)—*Continued*

IDENTIFICATION—Continued

12. At least one of the following is available for the identification of each virus for which services are offered.

E225

a. ORTHOMXYO (Influenza)-Hemagglutination inhibition (HI), Complement fixation (CF) Hemadsorption-inhibition test (HAdI) or Neutralization

b. PARAINFLUENZA-HAdI, CF, HI, or Neutralization

c. RESPIRATORY SYNCYTIAL VIRUS (RSV)-CF or Neutralization

d. MUMPS-HAdI, Neutralization, HI, or CF

e. MEASLES-Neutralization, HI, CF, or Fluorescent antibody (FA)

f. REOVIRUS-HI, CF, or Neutralization

g. ENTEROVIRUS (Polio, ECHO, Coxsackievirus) Neutralization, CF, HI, or FA

h. HERPES SIMPLEX, CYTOMEGALOVIRUS, VARICELLA (chicken pox), VARICELLA-ZOSTER-Neutralization, CF Passive hemagglutination test, HI, or Immuno-diffusion

i. CYTOMEGALOVIRUS (CMV)-Cytopathic effect (CPE), CF, or Neutralization

j.	VARICELLA-HERPES ZOSTER-Direct FA staining, Indirect staining, or CF					
k.	VARIOLA and VACCINA-Neutralization, CF, HI, Precipitation in agar gel or Passage with temperature challenge: Vaccina-40°C, Variola-36°C					
l.	ADENOVIRUS-Characteristic CPE, Retention of infectivity after exposure to ether or chloroform, Group-specific antigenicity, CF, Neutralization, or HI					
m.	RUBELLA-HI, Neutralization, CF, or Indirect FA					
n.	RHINOVIRUS-Neutralization					
o.	ARBOVIRUS-Inactivation by SDC (Sodium desoxycholate), Inactivation by ethyl ether or chloroform to distinguish from entero-virus, Neutralization, CF, or HI					
p.	RABIES VIRUS-Microscopic examination of mouse brain for Negri bodies, Rabies virus antigen by FRA (Fluorescent rabies antigen), or Cross-protection test.					

RECORDS

13. E132	a.	Records document the results of each step taken to obtain the patient final report.	74.50 405.1316
E154	b.	Daily accession assures proper identification of specimens throughout testing.	74.53 405.1316(f)
	c.	All records retained at least 2 years.	74.54(a) 405.1316(g)

147

Laboratory Code

	CFR No.	Yes	No	NA	Comments—Identify by Number
SYPHILIS SEROLOGY 74.22(c)-405.1317(b)(2)(iii)					
PREVENTIVE MAINTENANCE 74.20(a)-405.1317(a)(1)					
E177 1. There is a preventive maintenance program for each piece of equipment.	74.20(a)				
E132 2. Records are available to document preventive maintenance program is in operation and include:	.50 .20(f) .1316				
E132 a. Instrument name	.20(f) .1316				
E132 b. Date installed (if available)	.20(f) .1316				
E132 c. Serial number	.20(f) .1316				
E132 d. Number to call for service	.20(f) .1316				
E132 e. Date of service	.20(f) .1316				
E132 f. Nature of service	.20(f) .1316				
E132 g. Initials of person servicing	.20(f) .1316				
E132 h. Date of next service or service schedule	.20(f) .1316				

continued

Code	Item	Reference		
E132	i. Records of service	.20(f) .1316		
E233	2. The mechanical rotator is: a. Checked before each test run (VDRL 180(+)(−)3)(RPR 95−110)	74.22(c) 406.1317(b) (2)(ii)		
E132	b. Records document checks	74.50 405.1316		
E233	3. The needles are: a. Checked for accuracy each test run	74.22(c) 405.1317(a)(2) (ii)		
E132	b. Records document checks	74.50 405.1316		
E180	4. All remedial actions are taken to correct detected defects before patient results are reported. Recorded: Yes ___ No ___	.50 .20(f) .1317(a)(1)		

TEMPERATURES 74.20(b)-405.1317(a)(2)

Code	Item	Reference		
E187	5. The following temperature-controlled spaces and equipment are monitored each day of use to assure proper performance.	.20(b) .1317(a)(2)		
E187	a. Incubators	.20(b) .1317(a)(2)		
E187	b. Refrigerators	.20(b) .1317(a)(2)		
E187	c. Water baths	.20(b) .1317(a)(2)		

Laboratory Code

SYPHILIS SEROLOGY 74.22(c)-405.1317(b)(2)(iii)—*Continued*

TEMPERATURES 74.20(b)-405.1317(a)(2)—*Continued*

		CFR No.	Yes	No	NA	Comments–Identify by Number
E187	d. Heat blocks	.20(b) .1317(a)(2)				
E187	e. Freezers	.20(b) .1317(a)(2)				
E187	f. Ambient	.20(b) .1317(a)(2)				
E132	g. Recorded	74.50 405.1316				

INFORMATION

The laboratory performs the following syphilis serology:

		CFR No.	Yes	No	NA	Comments–Identify by Number
	a. VDRL					
	b. CSF VDRL					
	c. RPR 18mm Circle Card					
	d. ART					
	e. FTA-ABS					
	f. Other (Specify)					

REAGENTS 74.20(c)-405.1517(a)(3)

6. Reagents are properly labeled with:

		CFR No.	Yes	No	NA	Comments–Identify by Number
E188	a. Identity (name, lot number)	74.20(c) 405.1517(a)(3)				

E191	b.	A date (prepared, received, opened, or expiration)	.20(c)
E189	c.	Concentration, titer, or strength	.20(c)
E190	d.	Recommended storage requirements (if pertinent)	.20(c)
7. ANTIGEN:			
E233	a.	A new lot is compared with one standard reactivity before being placed in routine use.	74.22(c) 405.1317(b)(2) (iii)
E132	b.	Results recorded.	74.50 405.1316
E233	c.	VDRL antigen is used on the day of preparation only.	.22(c) .1317(b)(2) (iii)
E233	d.	CSF antigen is "sensitized" before use.	.22(c) .1317(b)(2) (iii)
8. CONTROL:			
E233	a.	A new lot is compared with one of standard reactivity before being placed in routine use.	.22(c) .1317(b)(2) (iii)
E132	b.	Results recorded.	74.50 405.1316
E233	c.	VDRL control is compared with a reference control before being placed in routine use.	.22(c) .1317(b)(2) (iii)

continued

SYPHILIS SEROLOGY 74.22(c)-405.1317(b)(2)(iii)—*Continued*

	CFR No.	Yes	No	NA	Comments—Identify by Number
REAGENTS 74.20(c)-405.1517(a)(3)—*Continued*					
9. Other Reagents:					
E233 New lots of the following are compared with one of standard reactivity before being placed in routine use.					
a. Conjugate	.22(c) .1317(b)(2) (iii)				
E233 b. Sorbent	.22(e) .1317(b)(2) (iii)				
E132 c. Results recorded	74.50 405.1316				
E233 New lots of conjugate are:					
a. Titered before being placed in routine use	.22(c) .1317(b)(2) (iii)				
E132 b. Results recorded	74.50 405.1316				
10. The laboratory does not use deteriorated	74.20(c)				
E192 materials or materials of substandard reactivity	405.1317(a)(3)				
STANDARD OPERATING PROCEDURE MANUAL 74.20(d)-405.1317(a)(4)					
11. A complete written description of methods in					
E193 use is in the immediate bench area and includes:	74.20(c) 405.1317(a)(4)				

Laboratory Code

continued

		Reference		
E194	a.	Analytical methods in use	.20(d) .1317(a)(4)	
E196	b.	Control procedures	.20(d) .1317(a)(4)	
E196	c.	Calibration procedures	.20(d) .1317(a)(4)	
E197	d.	Literature references	.20(d) .1317(a)(4)	
E195	e.	Reagents	.20(d) .1317(a)(4)	
E134	f.	An annual review and date by the technical supervisor	405.1316(a)	
E198	g.	Changes are initialed and dated by the technical supervisor	74.20(e) 405.1317(a)(5)	

STANDARD QUALITY CONTROL SYSTEM
74.22(c)-405.1317(b)(2)(iii)

	12.	Control sera of graded reactivity are included		
E233		each day of testing and include:	.22(c) .1317(b)(2) (iii)	
	a.	Nonreactive		
E233	b.	Weakly/minimally reactive	.22(c) .1317(b)(2) (iii)	
E233	c.	Reactive	.22(c) .1317(b)(2) (iii)	

SYPHILIS SEROLOGY 74.22(c)-
405.1317(b)(2)(iii)—*Continued*

STANDARD QUALITY CONTROL SYSTEM
74.22(c)-405.1317(b)(2)(iii)—*Continued*

	CFR No.	Yes	No	NA	Comments—Identify by Number
E132　d.　Results recorded	74.50 405.1316				
13.　The predetermined reactivity pattern of the control is obtained before test results are reported.	74.22(a) 405.1317(b)(i)				
14.　The following controls are included each time E233　tests are performed for FTA-ABS:	.22(c) .1317(b)(2) (iii)				
E233　a.　Reactive control serum in diluent					
E233　b.　Reactive control serum in sorbent	.22(c) .1317(b)(2) (iii)				
E233　c.　Minimally reactive control serum	.22(c) .1317(b)(2) (iii)				
E233　d.　Nonspecific serum control in diluent	.22(c) .1317(b)(2) (iii)				

154

Code	Item	Reference		
E233	e. Nonspecific serum control in sorbent	.22(c) .1317(b)(2) (iii)		
E233	f. Nonspecific staining control in diluent	.22(c) .1317(b)(2) (iii)		
E233	g. Nonspecific staining control in sorbent	.22(c) .1317(b)(2) (iii)		
E132	h. Results recorded	74.50 405.1316		

RECORDS

Code	Item	Reference		
E132	15. a. Records document the results of each step taken to obtain the patient final report.	74.50 405.1316		
E154	b. Daily accession assures proper identification of specimens throughout testing.	74.53 405.1316(f)		
E165	c. All records retained at least two years.	74.54(a) 405.1316(g)		

NON-SYPHILIS SEROLOGY 74.22(a)(b)
405.1317(b)(2)(i)

PREVENTIVE MAINTENANCE 74.20(a)-
405.1317(a)(1)(iii)

		CFR No.	Yes	NO	NA	Comments—Identify by Number
E177	1. There is a preventive maintenance program for each piece of equipment.	.20(a) .1317(a)(1)				
E132	Records are available to document that a preventive maintenance program is in operation and include:	.50 .20(f) .1316				
E132	a. Instrument name	.20(f) .1316				
E132	b. Date installed (if available)	.20(f) .1316				
E132	c. Serial number	.20(f) .1316				
E132	d. Number to call for service	.20(f) .1316				
E132	e. Date of service	.20(f) .1316				
E132	f. Nature of service	.20(f) .1316				
E132	g. Initials of person servicing	.20(f) .1316				
E132	h. Date of next service or service schedule	.20(f) .1316				

		Reference		
2.	All remedial actions are taken to correct detected defects before patient results are reported. Recorded: Yes ___ No ___	74.20(f) 405.1317(a)(21)		
E180				

TEMPERATURES 74.20(b)-405.1317(a)(2)

		Reference		
3.	The following temperature-controlled spaces and equipment are monitored each day of use to ensure proper performance:	74.20(b) 405.1317(a)(2)		
E187	a. Incubators	.20(b) .1317(a)(2)		
E187	b. Refrigerators	.20(b) .1317(a)(2)		
E187	c. Water baths	.20(b) .1317(a)(2)		
E187	d. Heat blocks	.20(b) .1317(a)(2)		
E187	e. Freezers	.20(b) .1317(a)(2)		
E187	f. Ambient	.20(b) .1317(a)(2)		
E132	g. Recorded	74.50 405.1316		

REAGENTS 74.20(c)-405.1517(a)(3)

		Reference		
4.	Reagents are properly labeled with:	.20(c) .1517(a)(3)		
E188	a. Identity (name, lot number)			

continued

	CFR No.	Yes	No	NA	Comments–Identify by Number

NON-SYPHILIS SEROLOGY 74.22(a)(b)
405.1317(b)(2)(i)—Continued

REAGENTS 74.20(c)-405.1517(a)(3)—Continued

	CFR No.	Yes	No	NA	Comments
E191 b. A date (prepared, received, opened, or expiration)	.20(c) .1517(a)(3)				
E189 c. Concentration, titer, or strength	.20(c) .1517(a)(3)				
E190 d. Recommended storage requirements (if pertinent)	.20(c) .1517(a)(3)				
5. Each new lot of the following is compared with one of acceptable reactivity before being placed in routine use: a. Reagents E232	74.22(b) 405.1317(b)(2) (ii)				
E232 b. Control material	.22(b) .1317(b)(2) (ii)				
E132 c. Results recorded	74.50 405.1316				
6. The laboratory does not use deteriorated materials or materials of substandard reactivity. E192	74.20(c) 405.1317(a)(3)				

STANDARD OPERATING PROCEDURE
MANUAL 74.20(d)-405.1317(a)(4)

	CFR No.	Yes	No	NA	Comments
7. A complete written description of methods in use is in the immediate bench area and includes: E193	.20(d) .1317(a)(4)				

158

Code		Description	Reference			
E194	a.	Analytical methods	.20(d)			
E196	b.	Control procedures	.20(d) .1317(a)(4)			
E196	c.	Calibration procedures	.20(d) .1317(a)(4)			
E197	d.	Literature references	.20(d) .1317(a)(4)			
E195	e.	Reagents	.20(d) .1317(a)(4)			
E134	f.	An annual review and date by the technical supervisor	.1316(a)			
E198	g.	Changes are initialed and dated by the technical supervisor	.20(e) .1317(a)(5)			

STANDARD QUALITY CONTROL SYSTEM
74.22(a)(b)-405.1317(b)(2)(i)(ii)

Code		Description	Reference			
	8.	Each qualitative test is run concurrently with a:				
E229	a.	Positive serum control	74.22(a)(b) 405.1317(b)(2) (i)			
E229	b.	Negative serum control	.22(a)(b) .1317(b)(2) (i)			

continued

NON-SYPHILIS SEROLOGY 74.22(a)(b) 405.1317(b)(2)(i)—*Continued*

STANDARD QUALITY CONTROL SYSTEM
74.22(a)(b)-405.1317(b)(2)(i)(ii)—*Continued*

		CFR No.	Yes	No	NA	Comments—Identify by Number
E132	c. Results recorded	74.50 74.20(f) 405.1316				
9.	Each quantitative test is run concurrently with a:					
E229	a. Positive serum control of graded reactivity	74.22(a)(b) 405.1317(b)(2) (i)(ii)				
E229	b. Negative serum control	.22(a)(b) .1317(b)(2) (i)(ii)				
E132	c. Results recorded	74.50 74.20(f) 405.1316				
10.	Controls for each individual test component are included for:					
E231	a. Complement fixation tests	74.22(a) 405.1317(b)(2) (i)				
E231	b. Hemagglutination-Inhibition tests	.22(a) .1317(b)(2) (i)				
11.	Test results are not reported unless the predetermined reactivity pattern of the control is obtained (i)	74.22(a)(b) 405.1317(b)(2) (i)				

12. RECORDS

E132	a.	Records document the results of each step taken to obtain the patient final report.	74.50 405.1316	
E154	b.	Daily accession assures proper identification specimens throughout testing.	74.53 405.1316(f)	
E165	c.	All records retained at least 2 years.	74.54(a) 405.1316(g)	

INFORMATION

The laboratory performs the following serology tests:

Qualitative

Febrile agglutination ☐
Mono Screen ☐
CRP ☐
LE ☐
ASO Screen ☐
ANA ☐
RA ☐
Other (specify)

Quantitative

Heterophile ☐
Presumptive ☐
ASO titer ☐
Rubella ☐
Hepatitis B ☐
Serum specific proteins ☐
IgA ☐ IgG ☐ IgM☐
Other (specify)

Differential ☐

	CFR No.	Yes	No	NA	Comments—Identify by Number
CLINICAL CHEMISTRY 74.23(a)-405.1317(b)(3)(i)					
PREVENTIVE MAINTENANCE 74.20(a)-405.1317(a)(1)					
1. There is a preventive maintenance program for each piece of equipment. E243 E177	.20(a) .1317(a)(10				
2. Records are available to document that a preventive maintenance program is in operation and include: E232 E132	74.50 74.20(f) 405.1316				
a. Instrument name					
b. Date installed (if available) E243 E132	.20(f) .1316				
c. Serial number E243 E132	.20(f) .1316				
d. Number to call for service E243 E132	.20(f) .1316				
e. Date of service E243 E132	.20(f) .1316				
f. Nature of service E243 E132	.20(f) .1316				
g. Initials of person servicing E243 E132	.20(f) .1316				
h. Date of next service or service schedule E243 E132	.20(f) .1316				

continued

	Item	Reference
E180	3. All remedial actions are taken to correct detected defects before patient results are reported. Recorded: Yes ___ No ___	74.50 74.20(f) 405.1317
E186 E240	4. Each instrument (or other device) is recalibrated or rechecked at least once each day of use for: a. All automated equipment	74.23(a) 405.1317(b)(3)(i)
E186	b. All manual testing equipment	.23(a) .1317(b)(3)(i)
E132	c. Results recorded	74.50 405.1316
E179	5. Volumetric equipment used for each method has been evaluated: a. Automated methods	74.20(a) 405.1317(a)(1) .20(a) .1317(a)(1)
E179	b. Manual methods	.20(a) .1317(a)(1)
E132	c. Results recorded	74.50 405.1316
E242	6. Records are maintained and are available to document:	74.20(a) 405.1317(a)(1)
E242	a. Routine precision of each automated method	
E240	b. Recalibration schedule of each automated method	.20(a) .1317(a)(1)

Laboratory Code

	CFR No.	Yes	No	NA	Comments–Identify by Number

CLINICAL CHEMISTRY
74.23(a)-405.1317(b)(3)(i)—*Continued*

PREVENTIVE MAINTENANCE 74.20(a)-
405.1317(a)(1)—*Continued*

		CFR No.	Yes	No	NA	Comments
E242	c. Routine precision of each manual method	.20(a) .1317(a)(1)				
E242	d. Recalibration schedule of each manual method	.20(a) .1317(a)(1)				
E135	7. For tests normally performed on automated test equipment, provision is made and documented for performing such tests by alternate methods in event equipment becomes inoperable.	405.1316(a)				

TEMPERATURES 74.20(b)-405.1317(a)(2)

E187	8. The following temperature-controlled spaces and equipment are monitored each day of use to assure proper performance.					
E187	a. Incubators	.20(b) .1317(a)(2)				
E187	b. Refrigerators	.20(b) .1317(a)(2)				
E187	c. Water baths	.20(b) .1317(a)(2)				
E187	d. Heat blocks	.20(b) .1317(a)(2)				

E187	e. Freezers	.20(b) .1317(a)(2)		
E187	f. Ambient	.20(b) .1317(a)(2)		
E132	g. Recorded	74.50 405.1316		

REAGENTS 74.20(c)-405.1517(a)(3)

	9. Reagents are properly labeled:			
E188	a. Identity (name, lot number)	74.20(c) 405.1517(a)(3)		
E191	b. A date (prepared, received, opened, or expiration)	.20(c) .1517(a)(3)		
E189	c. Concentration, titer, or strength	.20(c) .1517(a)(3)		
E190	d. Recommended storage requirements (if pertinent)	.20(c) .1517(a)(3)		
E192	10. The laboratory does not use deteriorated materials or materials of substandard reactivity	74.20(c) 405.1517(a)(3)		

STANDARD OPERATING PROCEDURE MANUAL 74.20(d)-405.1317(a)(4)

E193	11. A complete written description of methods in use is in the immediate bench area where personnel are engaged in examining specimens and includes:	74.20(d) 405.1317(a)(4)		
E194	a. Analytical methods in use	.20(d) .1317(a)(4)		

continued

CLINICAL CHEMISTRY
74.23(a)–405.1317(b)(3)(i)–*Continued*

STANDARD OPERATING PROCEDURE
MANUAL 74.20(d)–405.1317(a)(4)–*Continued*

	CFR No.	Yes	No	NA	Comments–Identify by Number
E196 b. Control procedures	.20(d) .1317(a)(4)				
E196 c. Calibration procedures	.20(d) .1317(a)(4)				
E195 d. Reagents	.20(d) .1317(a)(4)				
E197 e. Literature references	.20(d) .1317(a)(4)				
E134 f. Annual review and date by technical supervisor	.20(e) .1316(a)				
E198 g. Changes initialed and dated by technical supervisor	.1317(a)(5)				
12. The laboratory has a course of action to be E245 instituted when controls are outside of acceptable limits that is:	74.23(a) 405.1317(b)(3)(i)				
E245 a. Written	.23(a) .1317(b)(3)(i)				
E245 b. Followed	.23(a) .1317(b)(3)(i)				
E246 c. Documented	74.50 405.1316				

STANDARD QUALITY CONTROL SYSTEM
74.23(a)-405.1317(b)(3)(i)

13. Each test run of unknown samples includes at E244 least one standard and one control material *or* two levels of control material if a standard is not available	74.23(a) 405.1317(b)(3) (i)						
E244 a. Each automated run	.23(a) .1317(b)(3) (i)						
E244 b. Each manual run	.23(a) .1317(b)(3) (i)						
E132 c. Results recorded	74.50 405.1316						
14. Established limits are available and recorded for E245	74.50 405.1316						
E245 a. Standards used for automated tests	74.50 405.1316						
E245 b. Standards used for manual tests	74.50 405.1316						
E245 c. Control material used for automated tests	74.50 405.1316						
E245 d. Control material used for manual tests	74.50 405.1316						

continued

CLINICAL CHEMISTRY
74.23(a)-405.1317(b)(3)(i)—*Continued*

STANDARD QUALITY CONTROL SYSTEM
74.23(a)-405.1317(b)(3)(i)—*Continued*

	CFR No.	Yes	No	NA	Comments—Identify by Number
15. Electrophoretic procedures:					
E244 a. One control included with each run	.23(a) .1317(b)(3)(i)				
E132 b. Results recorded	74.50 405.1316				

RADIOIMMUNOASSAY TESTING

	CFR No.	Yes	No	NA	Comments—Identify by Number
16. Manufacturer's directions for use of commercial kits for radioimmunoassay procedures are followed by bench personnel *or* changes in manufacturer's technique have been validated by the laboratory.					
17. Counting equipment is:	74.20(b) 405.1317(a)(2)				
E240 E243 E186 a. Checked for stability with a radioactive standard each day of use					
E240 E243 E186 b. Checked for background stability each day of use					
E132 c. Results recorded	74.20(f) 405.1317(a)(b)				

168

PREGNANCY TESTING 74.23(a)-405.1317(b)(3)(i)

		Ref			
18.	Reagents used for pregnancy testing are tested when a new kit is opened and at least once per week of use with:				
E246	a. Positive control (urine/serum)	74.23(a) 405.1317(b)(3)(i)			
E246	b. Negative control (urine/serum)	.23(a) .1317(b)(3)(i)			
E132	c. Results recorded	74.50 405.1316			

DRUG TESTING 74.23(a)-405.1317(b)(3)(i)

19. E244	If the laboratory uses thin layer chromatography for drug screens a control material is processed in the exact manner as the unknown specimens.				
20. E244	If the laboratory uses a quantitative test for drugs or for the confirmation of screens a control material is processed in the exact manner as the unknown specimen.				
21. E241	Minimal detection limits have been established for each drug detected by the laboratory.				

RECORDS

E132	a. Records document the results of each step taken to obtain the patient final report.	74.50 405.1316			
E154	b. Daily accession assures proper identification of specimens throughout testing.	74.53 405.1316(f)			
E165	c. All records retained at least 2 years.	74.54 405.1316(g)			

169

CYTOGENETICS

PREVENTIVE MAINTENANCE 74.20(a)-
405.1317(a)(1)

		CFR No.	Yes	No	NA	Comments–Identify by Number
E177	1. There is a preventive maintenance program for each piece of equipment.	.20(a) .1317(a)(1)				
E132	2. Records are available to document that a preventive maintenance program is in operation and include:	.50 .20(f) .1316				
E132	a. Instrument name	.20(f) .1316				
E132	b. Date installed (if available)	.20(f) .1316				
E132	c. Serial number	.20(f) .1316				
E132	d. Number to call for service	.20(f) .1316				
E132	e. Date of service	.20(f) .1316				
E132	f. Nature of service	.20(f) .1316				
E132	g. Initials of person servicing	.20(f) .1316				
E132	h. Date of next service or service schedule	.20(f) .1316				

continued

E132	i. Results recorded	74.50 405.1316	
3.	All remedial actions are taken to correct detected defects before patient results are reported. Recorded: Yes ___ No ___	.50 .20(f) .1317	
E180			

TEMPERATURES 74.20(b)-405.1317(a)(2)

E187	4. The following temperature-controlled spaces and equipment are monitored each day of use to ensure proper performance:	.20(b) .1317(a)(2)	
E187	a. Incubators	.20(b) .1317(a)(2)	
E187	b. Refrigerators	.20(b) .1317(a)(2)	
E187	c. Water baths	.20(b) .1317(a)(2)	
E187	d. Heat blocks	.20(b) .1317(a)(2)	
E187	e. Freezers	.20(b) .1317(a)(2)	
E187	f. Ambient (when critical to test)	.20(b) .1317(a)(2)	
E132	g. Recorded	74.50 405.1316	

171

Laboratory Code

	CFR No.	Yes	No	NA	Comments–Identify by Number

CYTOGENETICS—*Continued*

REAGENTS 74.20(c)-405.1517(a)(3)

		CFR No.	Yes	No	NA	Comments
	5. All reagents are properly labeled					
E188	a. Identity (name, lot number)	.20(c) .1517(a)(3)				
E191	b. A date (prepared, received, opened, or expiration)	.20(c) .1517(a)(3)				
E189	c. Concentration, titer, or strength	.20(c) .1517(a)(3)				
	6. The laboratory does not use materials of					
E192	substandard reactivity or deteriorated material	.20(c) .1517(a)(3)				

STANDARD OPERATING PROCEDURE
MANUAL 74.20(d)-405.1317(a)(4)

		CFR No.	Yes	No	NA	Comments
E193	7. A complete written description of methods in use is in the immediate bench area where personnel are engaged in examining specimens.	.20(d) .1317(a)(4)				
E194	SOPM includes: a. Analytical methods in use	.20(d) .1317(a)(4)				
E196	b. Control procedures	.20(d) .1317(a)(4)				
E196	c. Calibration procedures	.20(d) .1317(a)(4)				
E195	d. Reagents	.20(d) .1317(a)(4)				

E197	e. Pertinent literature references	.20(d) .1317(a)(4)		
E134	f. Annual review and date by technical supervisor	.20(d) .1317(a)(4)		
E198	g. Changes initialed and dated by technical supervisor	.1317(a)(5)		

QUALITY CONTROL (74.29 CFR Tentative)

8. 1.	Sexchromatin determinations: a. A minimum of 100 cells are counted	74.29(a)(1)(i) (Tentative)		
	b. If less than 10 preparations per month for either x or y chromatin are examined, a positive chromatin control is included with each test run	74.29(a)(1) (ii) (Tentative)		
2.	Leukocyte and Fibroblast Cultures: a. A minimum of 10 cell spreads are counted	74.29(a)(2)(i) (Tentative)		
	b. A minimum of two cells are karyotyped	74.29(a)(2) (ii) (Tentative)		
	c. Records of karyotyping are maintained (the slides or photographs)	74.29(a)(2) (ii) (Tentative)		
3.	Amniotic fluid cultures: a. A minimum of 15 mitoses from two different containers are counted	74.29(a)(3) (ii) (Tentative)		

continued

Laboratory Code

CYTOGENETICS–*Continued*

QUALITY CONTROL (74.29 CFR Tentative)–*Continued*

	CFR No.	Yes	No	NA	Comments–Identify by Number
b. A minimum of two mitoses are karyotyped	74.29(a)(3) (ii) (Tentative)				
c. Records of karyotyping are maintained (the slides or photographs)	74.29(a)(3) (ii) (Tentative)				

RECORDS

	CFR No.	Yes	No	NA	Comments–Identify by Number
9. a. Records are maintained for all quality control procedures.	74.29(a)(4) (Tentative)				
b. Records document the results of each step taken to obtain the patient final report.	74.20 405.1316				
c. Daily accession assures proper identification of specimens throughout testing.	74.53 405.1316(f)				
d. All records are retained at least 2 years.	74.54(a) 405.1316(g)				

174

URINALYSIS 74.23(b)405.1317(b)(3iii)

PREVENTIVE MAINTENANCE 74.20(a)-405.1317(a)(1)

		CFR No.	Yes	No	NA	Comments—Identify by Number
E177	1. There is a preventive maintenance program for each piece of equipment.	74.20(a)				
E132	Records are available to document that a preventive maintenance program is in operation and include:	.50 .20(f) .1316				
E132	a. Instrument name	.20(f) .1316				
E132	b. Date installed (if available)	.20(f) .1316				
E132	c. Serial number	.20(f) .1316				
E132	d. Number to call for service	.20(f) .1316				
E132	e. Date of service	.20(f) .1316				
E132	f. Nature of service	.20(f) .1316				
E132	g. Initials of person servicing	.20(f) .1316				

continued

175

URINALYSIS 74.23(b)405.1317(b)(3)(iii)—*Continued*

PREVENTIVE MAINTENANCE 74.20(a)-405.1317(a)(1)—*Continued*

	CFR No.	Yes	No	NA	Comments—Identify by Number
E132 h. Date of next service or service schedule	.20(f) .1316				
E132 i. Results recorded	74.50 405.1316				
E180 2. All remedial actions are taken to correct detected defects before patient results are reported. Recorded: Yes____ No____	.50 .20(f) .1317(a)(1)				

TEMPERATURES 74.20(b)-405.1317(a)(2)

	CFR No.	Yes	No	NA	Comments—Identify by Number
E187 3. The following temperature-controlled spaces and equipment are monitored each day of use to ensure proper performance:	.20(b) .1317(a)(2)				
E187 a. Incubators	.20(b) .1317(a)(2)				
E187 b. Refrigerators	.20(b) .1317(a)(2)				
E187 c. Water baths	.20(b) .1317(a)(2)				
E187 d. Heat blocks	.20(b) .1317(a)(2)				

E187	e. Freezers	.20(b) .1317(a)(2)			
E187	f. Ambient (when critical to test)	.20(b) .1317(a)(2)			
E132	g. Recorded	74.50 405.1316			

REAGENTS 74.20(c)-405.1517(a)(3)

4. All reagents are properly labeled:

E188	a. Identity (name, lot number)	.20(c) .1517(a)(3)				
E191	b. A date (prepared, received, opened, or expiration)	.20(c) .1517(a)(3)				
E189	c. Concentration, titer, or strength	.20(c) .1517(a)(3)				
E190	d. Recommended storage requirements (if pertinent)	.20(c) .1517(a)(3)				
E192	5. The laboratory does not use deteriorated materials or materials of substandard reactivity					

STANDARD OPERATING PROCEDURE MANUAL 74.20(d)-405.1317(a)(4)

E193	6. A complete written description of methods in use is in the immediate bench area where personnel are engaged in examining specimens.	.20(c) .1317(a)(4)		

continued

URINALYSIS 74.23(b)405.1317(b)(3)(iii)—*Continued*

STANDARD OPERATING PROCEDURE MANUAL 74.20(d)-405.1317(a)(4)—*Continued*

	CFR No.	Yes	No	NA	Comments—Identify by Number
E194 SOPM includes:					
a. Analytical methods in use	.20(d) .1317(a)(4)				
E196 b. Control procedures	.20(d) .1317(a)(4)				
E196 c. Calibration procedures	.20(d) .1317(a)(4)				
E195 d. Reagents	.20(d) .1317(a)(4)				
E197 e. Pertinent literature references	.20(d) .1317(a)(4)				
E134 f. Annual review and date by technical supervisor	.1316(a)				
E198 g. Changes initialed and dated by technical supervisor	.1317(a)(5)				

QUALITY CONTROL

	CFR No.	Yes	No	NA	Comments—Identify by Number
7. All chemical urine procedures are checked each					
E247 day of use with a suitable reference sample	.23(b) .1317(b) (3iii)				
E248 a. Acceptable limits for reference sample are available	.23(b) .1317(b) (3iii)				

E132	b.	Reference sample recorded	.50 .1316		
E248	c.	Devices used to determine specific gravity are checked each day of use	.20(a) .1317(a)(1)		
E132	d.	Specific gravity checks are recorded	.50 .1316		

RECORDS

8. E132	a.	Records document the results of each step taken to obtain the patient final report	74.50 405.1316		
E154	b.	Daily accession ensures proper identification of specimens throughout testing	74.53 405.1316(f)		
E165	c.	All records retained at least 2 years	74.54(a) 405.1316(g)		

IMMUNOHEMATOLOGY 74.24-405.1317(b)(4)

PREVENTIVE MAINTENANCE 74.20(a)-
405.1317(a)(1)

	CFR No.	Yes	No	NA	Comments—Identify by Number
E177	1. There is a preventive maintenance program for each piece of equipment.	.20(a) .1317(a)(1)				
E243 E132	Records are available to document that a preventive maintenance program is in operation and include:405.1316	74.50 74.20(f) 405.1316				
	a. Instrument name					
E132	b. Date installed (if available)	.20(f) .1316				
E132	c. Serial number	.20(f) .1316				
E132	d. Number to call for service	.20(f) .1316				
E132	e. Date of service	.20(f) .1316				
E132	f. Nature of service	.20(f) .1316				
E132	g. Initials of person servicing	.20(f) .1316				
	h. Date of next service or service schedule	.20(f) .1316				

continued

	74.50 74.20(f) 405.1317	

2. All remedial actions are taken to correct
E180 detected defects before patient results are
reported.
Recorded: Yes ___ No ___

TEMPERATURES 74.20(b)-405.1317(a)(2)

3. The following temperature-controlled spaces and E187 equipment are monitored each day of use to ensure proper performance:	.20(b) .1317(a)(2)	
E187 a. Incubators	.20(b) .1317(a)(2)	
E187 b. Refrigerators	.20(b) .1317(a)(2)	
E187 c. Water baths	.20(b) .1317(a)(2)	
E187 d. Heat blocks	.20(b) .1317(a)(2)	
E187 e. Freezers	.20(b) .1317(a)(2)	
E187 f. Ambient	.20(b) .1317(a)(2)	
E132 g. Recorded	74.50 405.1316	

181

IMMUNOHEMATOLOGY 74.24-405.1317(b)(4)—*Continued*

STANDARD OPERATING PROCEDURE MANUAL 74.20(d)-405.1317(a)(4)

	CFR No.	Yes	No	NA	Comments–Identify by Number
E193	4. A complete written description of methods in use is in the immediate bench area where personnel are engaged in examining specimens and includes:	74.20(d) 405.1317(a)(4)				
E194	a. Analytical methods in use	.20(d) .1317(a)(4)				
E196	b. Control procedures	.20(d) .1317(a)(4)				
E196	c. Calibration procedures	.20(d) .1317(a)(4)				
E195	d. Reagents	.20(d) .1317(a)(4)				
E197	e. Pertinent literature reference	.20(d) .1317(a)(4)				
E134	f. Annual review and date by technical supervisor	.20(e) .1316(a)				
E198	g. Changes initialed and dated by technical supervisor	.1317(a)(5)				

REAGENTS 74.20(c)-405.1517(a)(3)

5. Reagents are properly labeled:	74.20(c)	
E188 a. Identity (name, lot number)	405.1517(a)(3)	
E191 b. A date (prepared, received, opened, or expiration)	.20(c) .1517(a)(3)	
E189 c. Concentration, titer, or strength	.20(c) .1517(a)(3)	
E190 d. Recommended storage requirements (if pertinent)	.20(c) .1517(a)(3)	
6. The laboratory does not use deteriorated E192 materials or materials of substandard reactivity	74.20(c) 405.1517(a)(3)	
7. All antisera in use in the laboratory are licensed E250 under Part 610, Section 21, Code of Federal E251 Regulations or possess equivalent potency.	74.24 405.1317(b)(4)	

ABO GROUPING

8. The ABO grouping is performed by testing:	74.24	
E250 a. Unknown RBC with Anti-A	405.1317(b)(4)	
E250 b. Unknown RBC with Anti-B	.24 .1317(b)(4)	
9. The ABO grouping is confirmed by testing:	.24	
E250 a. Unknown serum with known A red cells	.1317(b)(4)	
E250 b. Unknown serum with known B red cells	.24 .1317(b)(4)	

continued

183

Laboratory Code

	CFR No.	Yes	No	NA	Comments—Identify by Number

IMMUNOHEMATOLOGY 74.24-405.1317(b)(4)—Continued

ABO GROUPING—Continued

	CFR No.	Yes	No	NA	Comments—Identify by Number
10. The technique in use for ABO grouping is the technique for which the antisera are specifically designed to be effective.	.24 .1317(b)(4)				

RH_0 (D) TYPE

	CFR No.	Yes	No	NA	Comments—Identify by Number
11. The Rh_0 (D) type is performed by testing E251 unknown RBC with Anti-Rh_0 (D).	74.24-405.1317(b)(4)				
12. A control system of patient's RBC suspended in E253 his own serum or albumin is employed with each test.	.24 .1317(b)(4)				
13. All Rh_0 (D) negative RBC are tested for the Rh_0 E252 (D) variant D^u.	.24 .1317(b)(4)				
14. The technique in use for Rh_0 (D) typing is the E251 technique for which the antisera are specifically designed to be effective.	.24 .1317(b)(4)				

QUALITY CONTROL

	CFR No.	Yes	No	NA	Comments—Identify by Number
15. The reliability of each vial of reagent is tested E254 each day of use with:	.24 .1317(b)(4)				
a. A known negative control					
b. A known positive control E254	.24 .1317(b)(4)				
16. The reliability of each vial of cells is tested each E254 day of use with:	.24 .1317(b)(4)				

	Reference		
a. A known negative control	.24		
E254 b. A known positive control	.1317(b)(4)		

ANTIBODY INFORMATION ONLY

17. The laboratory offers the services of:			
a. Antibody detection			
b. Antibody identification			
c. Antibody titrations			

COMPATIBILITY TESTING INFORMATION ONLY

18. The laboratory offers compatibility testing service.			
19. Compatibility procedure includes:			
a. Major–saline			
b. Major–albumin			
c. Major–Coombs			
d. Minor			
e. Antibody detection (recipient)			
f. Autocontrol (recipient)			

RECORDS 74.50-405.1316

20. Records document the results of each step E132 taken to obtain the patient final report for:	74.50 405.1316		
E132 a. ABO direct cell grouping	.50 .1316		

continued

IMMUNOHEMATOLOGY 74.24-405.1317(b)(4)–*Continued*

RECORDS 74.50-405.1316–*Continued*

	CFR No.	Yes	No	NA	Comments–Identify by Number
E132 b. ABO reverse cell confirmation	.50 .1316				
E132 c. Anti-Rh_o (D) type	.50 .1316				
E132 d. Autologous cell control	.50 .1316				
E132 e. D^u testing	.50 .1316				
E132 f. Antibody screening	.50 .1316				
E132 g. Antibody identification	.50 .1316				
E132 h. Compatibility testing	.50 .1316				
21. Records document quality control for each vial of:					
E132 a. Reagents	.50 .1316				
E132 b. Cells	.50 .1316				
22. Daily accession assures proper E154 identification of specimens throughout testing	74.53 405.1316(f)				
23. All records retained at least 2 years E165	74.54(a) 405.1316(g)				

HEMATOLOGY 74.25-405.1317(b)(5)

PREVENTIVE MAINTENANCE 74.20(a)-405.1317(a)(1)

		CFR No.	Yes	No	NA	Comments– Identify by Number
	1. There is a preventive maintenance program for each piece of equipment.	.20(a) .1317(a)(1)				
E132	Records are available to document that a preventive maintenance program is in operation and include:	74.20(f) 74.50 405.1316				
E132	a. Instrument name	.20(f) .1316				
E132	b. Date installed (if available)	.20(f) .1316				
E132	c. Serial number	.20(f) .1316				
E132	d. Number to call for service	.20(f) .1316				
E132	e. Date of service	.20(f) .1316				
E132	f. Nature of service	.20(f) .1316				
E132	g. Initials of person servicing	.20(f) .1316				
E132	h. Date of next service or service schedule	.20(f) .1316				

continued

187

HEMATOLOGY 74.25-405.1317(b)(5)—*Continued*

PREVENTIVE MAINTENANCE 74.20(a)-405.1317(a)(1)—*Continued*

	CFR No.	Yes	No	NA	Comments—Identify by Number
2. All remedial actions are taken to correct detected defects before patient results are reported. Recorded: Yes ___ No ___ E180	74.20(a) 405.1317				
3. There is periodic inspection or testing for proper operation of equipment and instruments.					
E179 a. Volumetric equipment is evaluated.	74.20(a) 405.1317(a)(1)				
E132 b. Records document operation checks.	74.20(a) 405.1317(a)(1)				
E132 c. Records document volumetric checks.	74.20(f) 405.1317(a)(1)				
	74.20(f) 405.1317(a)(1)				

TEMPERATURES 74.20(b)-405.1317(a)(2)

	CFR No.	Yes	No	NA	Comments—Identify by Number
4. The following temperature-controlled spaces and equipment are monitored each day of use to ensure proper performance: E187	74.20(b) 405.1317(a)(2)				
E187 a. Refrigerators	.20(b) .1317(a)(2)				
E187 b. Water baths	.20(b) .1317(a)(2)				
E187 c. Heat blocks	.20(b) .1317(a)(2)				
E187 d. Recorded	.20 .1316				

REAGENTS 74.20(c)-405.1317(a)(3)

5. All reagents are properly labeled: E188	74.20(c) 405.1317(a)(3)		
E188 a. Identity (name, lot number)			
E191 b. A date (prepared, received, opened, or expiration)	.20(c) .1317(a)(3)		
E189 c. Concentration, titer, or strength	.20(c) .1317(a)(3)		
E190 d. Recommended storage requirements (if pertinent)	.20(c) .1317(a)(3)		
6. Reagents used for each method (automated or E179 manual) are evaluated before use.	74.20(a) 405.1317(a)(1)		
7. Standards and controls used for each method are E179 evaluated before use.	74.20(a) 405.1317(a)(1)		
8. Records document: E132	74.20(f) 405.1317(a)(6)		
E132 a. Reagent evaluation	74.20(f) .1317(a)(6)		
E132 b. Standard evaluation	74.20(f) .1317(a)(6)		
E132 c. Control evaluation	74.20(f) .1317(a)(6)		
9. The laboratory does not use deteriorated E192 material or material of substandard reactivity.	74.20(c) 405.1317(a)(3)		

continued

189

HEMATOLOGY 74.25-405.1317(b)(5)—*Continued*

STANDARD OPERATING PROCEDURE
MANUAL 74.20(d)-405.1317(a)(4)

		CFR No.	Yes	No	NA	Comments—Identify by Number
10.	A complete written description of methods in	74.20(d)				
E193	use is in the immediate bench area where	405.1317(a)(4)				
	personnel are engaged in examining specimens.					
	SOPM includes:					
E194	a. Analytical methods in use	74.20 405.1317(a)(4)				
E196	b. Control procedures	.20(a) .1317(a)(4)				
E196	c. Calibration procedures	.20(a) .1317(a)(4)				
E195	d. Reagents	.20(a) .1317(a)(4)				
E197	e. Literature references	.20(a) .1317(a)(4)				
E134	f. Annual review and date by technical supervisor	405.1316(a)				
E198	g. Changes initialed and dated by technical supervisor	74.20 405.1317(a)(5)				

AUTOMATED QUALITY CONTROL

11. Each instrument or procedure is checked or recalibrated each day of use for:

	RBC	WBC	HGB	HCT	
E256					74.25 .1317(b)(5)
E258 E256	a. Accuracy (with standards or controls that cover the entire range of expected values)				74.25 405.1317(b)(5)
E266	b. Precision (with an additional control or replicate testing of specimens)				74.25 405.1317(b)(5)
E132	c. Records document accuracy				74.50 405.1316
E265	d. Statistical estimates of precision are available				74.25 405.1317(b)(5)
E135	e. Provision is made for performing automated test by alternate methods if equipment is inoperable				405.1316(a)

continued

	CFR No.	Yes	No	NA	Comments—Identify by Number

HEMATOLOGY 74.25-405.1317(b)(5)—*Continued*

MANUAL QUALITY CONTROL

	CFR No.	Yes	No	NA	Comments—Identify by Number
12. Instruments and devices used for specimen examination are recalibrated, retested, or reinspected each day of use. Recorded: Yes ___ No ___	74.25 405.1317(b)(5)				
13. Each procedure is rechecked each day of use with standards or controls: RBC ___ WBC ___ HGB ___ HCT ___ Recorded: Yes ___ No ___	74.25 405.1317(b)(5)				

BLOOD FILM

	CFR No.	Yes	No	NA	Comments—Identify by Number
14. Patient blood films are: a. Clearly labeled for identification					
b. Properly prepared					
c. Properly stained					
d. Abnormal films read by pathologist or supervisory technologist					
e. At least 100 cells counted routinely					
f. Report includes RBC evaluation					
g. Report includes platelet evaluation					

COAGULATION

	CFR No.	Yes	No	NA	Comments—Identify by Number
15. Prothrombin time: a. Run in duplicate	74.25 405.1317(b)(5)				

		Reference	
E260	b. Controls covering entire range of expected values are run each day the test is performed	74.20	405.1317(b)(5)
E260	c. Control material recorded	74.50	405.1316
16.	Other coagulation testing:		
E260	a. A control material included each test run (as may be appropriate)	74.25	405.1317(b)(5)
E132	b. Control material recorded	74.20	405.1316
17. E259	A course of action to be instituted when standard or controls are outside acceptable limits is:	74.20	405.1317(a)(1)
E259	a. Written	.23(a)	.1317(b)(3)(i)
E259	b. Followed	.23(a)	.1317(b)(3)(i)
E259	c. Documented	74.50	405.1316

RECORDS

18. E246	a. Records document the results of each step taken to obtain the patient final report	74.50	
E132 E154	b. Daily accession ensures proper identification of specimens throughout testing	74.53	405.1316(f)
E165	c. All records retained at least 2 years	74.54(a)	405.1316(g)

193

CYTOLOGY 74.26(a)-405.1317(b)(6i)

PREVENTIVE MAINTENANCE 74.20(a)-405.1317(a)(1)

		CFR No.	Yes	No	NA	Comments–Identify by Number
E177	1. There is a preventive maintenance program for each piece of equipment.	74.20(a) 405.1317(a)(1)				
E132	2. Records are available to document that a preventive maintenance program is in operation and include:	.50 .20(f) .1316				
E132	a. Instrument name	.20(f) .1316				
E132	b. Date installed (if available)	74.20(f) .1316				
E132	c. Serial number	.20(f) .1316				
E132	d. Number to call for service	.20(f) .1316				
E132	e. Date of service	.20(f) .1316				
E132	f. Nature of service	.20(f) .1316				
E132	g. Initials of person servicing	.20(f) .1316				

continued

E132	h. Date of next service or service schedule	.20(f) .1316			
E132	i. Results recorded	74.50 405.1316			
E180	2. All remedial actions are taken to correct detected defects before patient results are reported. Recorded: Yes ___ No ___	.50 .20(f) .1317(a)(1)			

TEMPERATURES 74.20(b)-405.1317(a)(2)

E187	3. The following temperature-controlled spaces and equipment are monitored each day of use to ensure proper performance:	.20(b) .1317(a)(2)			
E187	a. Incubators	.20(b) .1317(a)(2)			
E187	b. Refrigerators	.20(b) .1317(a)(2)			
E187	c. Water baths	.20(b) .1317(a)(2)			
E187	d. Heat blocks	.20(b) .1317(a)(2)			
E187	e. Freezers	.20(b) .1317(a)(2)			
E187	f. Ambient (when critical to test)	.20(b) .1317(a)(2)			
E132	g. Recorded	74.50 405.1316			

Laboratory Code

CYTOLOGY 74.26(a)-405.1317(b)(6i)—*Continued*

REAGENTS 74.20(c)-405.1517(a)(3)

	CFR No.	Yes	No	NA	Comments–Identify by Number
4. All reagents are properly labeled:					
E188 a. Identity (name, lot number)	.20(c) .1517(a)(3)				
E191 b. A date (prepared, received, opened, or expiration)	.20(c) .1517(a)(3)				
E189 c. Concentration, titer, or strength	.20(c) .1517(a)(3)				
E190 d. Recommended storage requirements (if pertinent)	.20(c) .1517(a)(3)				
5. The laboratory does not use materials					
E192 of substandard reactivity or deteriorated material.	.20(c) .1517(a)(3)				

STANDARD OPERATING PROCEDURE MANUAL 74.20(d)-405.1317(a)(4)

	CFR No.	Yes	No	NA	Comments–Identify by Number
6. A complete written description of methods in					
E193 use is in the immediate bench area where personnel are engaged in examining specimens.	.20(d) .1317(a)(4)				
E194 SOPM includes: a. Analytical methods in use	.20(d) .1317(a)(4)				
E196 b. Control procedures	.20(d) .1317(a)(4)				

E196	c. Calibration procedures	.20(d) .1317(a)(4)		
E195	d. Reagents	.20(d) .1317(a)(4)		
E197	e. Pertinent literature references	.20(d) .1317(a)(4)		
E134	f. Annual review and date by technical supervisor	.20(e) .1316(a)		
E198	g. Changes initialed and dated by technical supervisor	.1317(a)(5)		

QUALITY CONTROL 74.26(a)-405.1317(b)(6i)

E274	7. All gynecological smears interpreted to be in the suspicious or positive categories by screeners are confirmed by the laboratory director or a qualified supervisor.	74.26(a) 405.1317(b)(6i)		
E273	8. A random sample of at least 10% of gynecological smears interpreted to be in one of the benign categories by screeners not qualified as supervisor or director are rescreened by personnel qualified as supervisor or director.	74.26(a) 405.1317(b)(6i)		
E274	9. All nongynecological cytological preparations, positive and negative, are reviewed by a director or supervisor qualified in cytology.	74.26(a) 405.1317(b)(6i)		

continued

197

Laboratory Code

CYTOLOGY 74.26(a)–405.1317(b)(6i)—*Continued*

RECORDS AND REPORTS

		CFR No.	Yes	No	NA	Comments—Identify by Number
10.	a. Records of the 10% rescreen are maintained and are available.					
E132		74.50 405.1316				
E274	b. Reports of all gynecological smears interpreted to be suspicious or positive are signed by a physician qualified in pathology or cytology.	74.26(a) 405.1317(b)(6i)				
E276	c. Cytology reports utilize an established nomenclature.	74.54(b)				
E277	d. All smears are retained for at least two years from date of examination.	74.26(a) 405.1317(b)(6i)				
E154	e. Daily accession assures proper identification of specimens throughout testing.	74.53 405.1316(f)				

HISTOLOGY 74.26(b)-405.1317(b)(6ii)

PREVENTIVE MAINTENANCE 74.20(a)-405.1317(a)(1)

		CFR No.	Yes	No	NA	Comments—Identify by Number
E177	1. There is a preventive maintenance program for each piece of equipment.	74.20(a) 405.1317(a)(1)				
E132	Records are available to document that a preventive maintenance program is in operation and include:	.50 .20(f) .1316				
E132	a. Instrument name	.20(f) .1316				
E132	b. Date installed (if available)	74.20(f) .1316				
E132	c. Serial number	.20(f) .1316				
E132	d. Number to call for service	.20(f) .1316				
E132	e. Date of service	.20(f) .1316				
E132	f. Nature of service	.20(f) .1316				
E132	g. Initials of person servicing	.20(f) .1316				

continued

Laboratory Code

	CFR No.	Yes	No	NA	Comments–Identify by Number

HISTOLOGY 74.26(b)-405.1317(b)(6ii)—*Continued*

PREVENTIVE MAINTENANCE 74.20(a)-
405.1317(a)(1)—*Continued*

		CFR No.	Yes	No	NA	Comments
E132	h. Date of next service or service schedule	.20(f) .1316				
E132	i. Results recorded	74.50 405.1316				
E180	2. All remedial actions are taken to correct detected defects before patient results are reported. Recorded: Yes __ No __	.50 .20(f) .1317(a)(1)				

TEMPERATURES 74.20(b)-405.1317(a)(2)

		CFR No.	Yes	No	NA	Comments
E187	3. The following temperature-controlled spaces and equipment are monitored each day of use to ensure proper performance:	.20(b) .1317(a)(2)				
E187	a. Incubators	.20(b) .1317(a)(2)				
E187	b. Refrigerators	.20(b) .1317(a)(2)				
E187	c. Water baths	.20(b) .1317(a)(2)				
E187	d. Heat blocks	.20(b) .1317(a)(2)				

E187	e. Freezers	.20(b) .1317(a)(2)		
E187	f. Ambient (when critical to test)	.20(b) .1317(a)(2)		
E132	g. Recorded	74.50 405.1316		

REAGENTS 74.20(c)-405.1517(a)(3)

	4. All reagents are properly labeled:			
E188	a. Identity (name, lot number)	.20(c) .1517(a)(3)		
E191	b. A date (prepared, received, opened, or expiration)	.20(c) .1517(a)(3)		
E189	c. Concentration, titer, or strength	.20(c) .1517(a)(3)		
E190	d. Recommended storage requirements (if pertinent)	.20(c) .1517(a)(3)		
E192	5. The laboratory does not use materials of substandard reactivity or deteriorated material	.20(c) .1517(a)(3)		

STANDARD OPERATING PROCEDURE MANUAL 74.20(d)-405.1317(a)(4)

E193	6. A complete written description of methods in use is in the immediate bench area where personnel are engaged in examining specimens.	.20(d) .1317(a)(4)		

continued

HISTOLOGY 74.26(b)–405.1317(b)(6ii)–Continued

STANDARD OPERATING PROCEDURE MANUAL 74.20(d)–405.1317(a)(4)–Continued

		CFR No.	Yes	No	NA	Comments–Identify by Number
E194	SOPM includes: a. Analytical methods in use	.20(d) .1317(a)(4)				
E196	b. Control procedures	.20(d) .1317(a)(4)				
E196	c. Calibration procedures	.20(d) .1317(a)(4)				
E195	d. Reagents	.20(d) .1317(a)(4)				
E197	e. Pertinent literature references	.20(d) .1317(a)(4)				
E132	f. Annual review and date by technical supervisor	.20(e) .1316(a)				
E198	g. Changes initialed and dated by technical supervisor	.1317(a)(5)				

QUALITY CONTROL 74.26(b)–405.1317(b)(6ii)

		CFR No.	Yes	No	NA	Comments–Identify by Number
E279	7. All special stains are controlled for intended reactivity by use of positive slides.	.26(b) .1317(b)(6ii)				
E280	8. Stained slides are retained for at least two years from date of examination.	.26(b) .1317(b)(6ii)				

#		Requirement	Reference		
9.	E280	Tissue blocks are retained for at least one year from date of examination.		.26(b) .1317(b)(6ii)	
10.	E281	Remnants of tissue specimens are retained in a fixative solution until those portions submitted for microscopy have been examined and a diagnosis made by a pathologist.		.26(b) .1317(b)(6ii)	

RECORDS AND REPORTS

#		Requirement	Reference		
11.	E168	Tissue pathology reports utilize terminology of a recognized system of disease nomenclature.		405.1316(g)(3)	
12.	E132	Stain control slides are documented.		.50 .1316	
13.	E154	Daily accession ensures proper identification of specimens throughout testing.		74.53 405.1316(f)	
14.	E165	All records are retained at least 2 years.		74.54(a) 405.1316(g)	

	CFR No.	Yes	No	NA	Comments–Identify by Number
RADIOBIOASSAY 74.27-405.1317(b)(7)					
PREVENTIVE MAINTENANCE 74.20(a)-405.1317(a)(1)					
1. There is a preventive maintenance program for each piece of equipment. E177	74.20(a) 405.1317(a)(1)				
E132 Records are available to document that a preventive maintenance program is in operation and include:	.50 .20(f) .1316				
E132 a. Instrument name	.20(f) .1316				
E132 b. Date installed (if available)	74.20(f) .1316				
E132 c. Serial number	.20(f) .1316				
E132 d. Number to call for service	.20(f) .1316				
E132 e. Date of service	.20(f) .1316				
E132 f. Nature of service	.20(f) .1316				
E132 g. Initials of person servicing	.20(f) .1316				
E132 h. Date of next service or service schedule	.20(f) .1316				
E132 i. Results recorded	74.50 405.1316				

204

2. E180	All remedial actions are taken to correct detected defects before patient results are reported.	.50 .20(f) .1317	

TEMPERATURES 74.20(b)-405.1317(a)(2)

3. E187	The following temperature-controlled spaces and equipment are monitored each day of use to ensure proper performance:	.20(b) .1317(a)(2)	
E187	a. Incubators	.20(b) .1317(a)(2)	
E187	b. Refrigerators	.20(b) .1317(a)(2)	
E187	c. Water baths	.20(b) .1317(a)(2)	
E187	d. Heat blocks	.20(b) .1317(a)(2)	
E187	e. Freezers	.20(b) .1317(a)(2)	
E187	f. Ambient (when critical to test)	.20(b) .1317(a)(2)	
E132	g. Recorded	74.50 405.1316	

REAGENTS 74.20(c)-405.1517(a)(3)

4. E188	All reagents are properly labeled: a. Identity (name, lot number)	.20(c) .1517(a)(3)	
E191	b. A date (prepared, received, opened, or expiration)	.20(c) .1517(a)(3)	

continued

	CFR No.	Yes	No	NA	Comments–Identify by Number
RADIOBIOASSAY 74.27-405.1317(b)(7)—*Continued*					
REAGENTS 74.20(c)-405.1517(a)(3)—*Continued*					
E189 c. Concentration, titer, or strength	.20(c) .1517(a)(3)				
E190 d. Recommended storage requirements (if pertinent)	.20(c) .1517(a)(3)				
5. The laboratory does not use materials					
E192 of substandard reactivity or deteriorated material	.20(c) .1517(a)(3)				
STANDARD OPERATING PROCEDURE MANUAL 74.20(d)-405.1317(a)(4)					
6. A complete written description of methods in					
E193 use is in the immediate bench area where personnel are engaged in examining specimens	.20(d) .1317(a)(4)				
E194 SOPM includes:					
a. Analytical methods in use	.20(d) .1317(a)(4)				
E196 b. Control procedures	.20(d) .1317(a)(4)				
E196 c. Calibration procedures	.20(d) .1317(a)(4)				
E195 d. Reagents	.20(d) .1317(a)(4)				
E197 e. Pertinent literature references	.20(d) .1317(a)(4)				

E134	f. Annual review and date by technical supervisor	.20(e) .1316(a)
E198	g. Changes initialed and dated by technical supervisor	.1317(a)(5)

QUALITY CONTROL 74.27-405.1317(b)(7)

E283	7. Counting equipment is checked for stability at least once on each day of use with radioactive standards or reference source	.27 .1317(b)(7)
E283	For each method there are established: a. The routine precision	.27 .1317(b)(7)
E283	b. The recalibration schedule	.27 .1317(b)(7)

RECORDS AND REPORTS

E132	8. Results of equipment stability checks are recorded	74.20(f) 74.50 405.1316
E285	For each method records are available with document: a. The routine precision	74.50 .1316
E285	b. The recalibration schedule	74.50 .1316
E132	9. Records document the results of each step taken to obtain the patient final result.	74.50 405.1316
E154	10. Daily accession ensures proper identification of specimens throughout testing.	74.53 405.1316(f)
E165	11. All records are retained at least 2 years.	74.54(a) 405.1316(g)

Laboratory Code

HISTOCOMPATIBILITY 405.1317(b)(8)

PREVENTIVE MAINTENANCE 74.20(a)
405.1317(a)(1)

		CFR No.	Yes	No	NA	Comments—Identify by Number
1.	There is a preventive maintenance program for	74.20(a)				
E177	each piece of equipment.	405.1317(a)(1)				
E132	Records are available to document that a preventive maintenance program is in operation and include:	.50 .20(f) .1316				
E132	a. Instrument name	.20(f) .1316				
E132	b. Date installed (if available)	74.20(f) .1316				
E132	c. Serial number	.20(f) .1316				
E132	d. Number to call for service	.20(f) .1316				
E132	e. Date of service	.20(f) .1316				
E132	f. Nature of service	.20(f) .1316				
E132	g. Initials of person servicing	.20(f) .1316				

E132	h. Date of next service or service schedule	.20(f) .1316		
E132	i. Results recorded	74.50 405.1316		
E180	2. All remedial actions are taken to correct detected defects before patient results are reported.	.50 .20(f) .1317		

TEMPERATURES 74.20(b)-405.1317(a)(2)

E187	3. The following temperature-controlled spaces and equipment are monitored each day of use to ensure proper performance:					
E187	a. Incubators	.20(b) .1317(a)(2)				
E187	b. Refrigerators	.20(b) .1317(a)(2)				
E187	c. Water baths	.20(b) .1317(a)(2)				
E187	d. Heat blocks	.20(b) .1317(a)(2)				
E187	e. Freezers	.20(b) .1317(a)(2)				
E187	f. Ambient (when critical to test)	.20(b) .1317(a)(2)				
E132	g. Recorded	74.50 405.1316				

continued

Laboratory Code

	CFR No.	Yes	No	NA	Comments—Identify by Number

HISTOCOMPATIBILITY 450.1317(b)(8)—*Continued*

REAGENTS 74.20(c)-405.1517(a)(3)

		CFR No.			
E188	4. All reagents are properly labeled:	.20(c) .1517(a)(3)			
E191	a. Identity (name, lot number) b. A date (prepared, received, opened, or expiration)	.20(c) .1517(a)(3)			
E189	c. Concentration, titer, or strength	.20(c) .1517(a)(3)			
E190	d. Recommended storage requirements (if pertinent)	.20(c) .1517(a)(3)			
R192	The laboratory does not use deteriorated materials or materials of substandard reactivity.	.20(c) .1517(2)(3)			
E250 E251	All antisera in use in the laboratory are licensed under Part 610, Title 21, Code of Federal Regulations, or possess equivalent potency.	74.24 405.1317(b)(4)			

STANDARD OPERATING PROCEDURE MANUAL 74.20(d)-405.1317(a)(4)

E193	5. A complete written description of methods in use is in the immediate bench area where personnel are engaged in examining specimens.	.20(d) .1317(a)(4)			

E194	SOPM includes:			
	a. Analytical methods in use	.20(d) .1317(a)(4)		
E196	b. Control procedures	.20(d) .1317(a)(4)		
E196	c. Calibration procedures	.20(d) .1317(a)(4)		
E195	d. Reagents	.20(d) .1317(a)(4)		
E197	e. Pertinent literature references	.20(d) .1317(a)(4)		
E134	f. Annual review and date by technical supervisor	.20(e) .1316(a)		
E198	g. Changes initialed and dated by technical supervisor	.1317(a)(5)		

GENERAL QUALITY CONTROL
405.1317(b)(8)

6. To verify each individual's ability to reproduce test results at least once per month, each individual performing testing is given a previously tested specimen as an unknown.	405.1317(b)(8)			
Results recorded	74.50 .1316			
7. The laboratory participates in a cell exchange program with another laboratory or a national or regional cell exchange program.	.1317(b)(8)			

continued

HISTOCOMPATIBILITY 405.1317(b)(8)—*Continued*

GENERAL QUALITY CONTROL
405.1317(b)(8)—*Continued*

	CFR No.	Yes	No	NA	Comments—Identify by Number
8. Incompletely characterized lymphocytes are retyped when antisera from new specificities become available.	.1317(b)(8)				
Results recorded	74.50 405.1316				
9. Each new lot of complement is tested for inherent toxicity prior to use with a:					
a. Positive control	.1317(b)(8)				
b. Negative control	.1317(b)(8)				
c. Results recorded	74.50 405.1316				
10. Test cells are tested for viability prior to or concurrently with use.	.1317(b)(8)				
Results recorded	74.50 405.1316				

RECORDS

	CFR No.	Yes	No	NA	Comments—Identify by Number
11. a. Records document the results of each step taken to obtain the patient result.	74.50 405.1316				
b. Daily accession ensures proper identification of specimens throughout testing.	74.53 405.1316(f)				
c. All records are retained at least 2 years.	74.54(a) 405.1316(g)				

IMMUNOHEMATOLOGY 74.24-405.1317(b)(4)

12. The ABO grouping is performed by testing:	.24 .1317(b)(4)			
a. Unknown RBC with Anti-A	.24 .1317(b)(4)			
b. Unknown RBC with Anti-B				
c. Results recorded	74.50 405.1316			
13. The ABO grouping is confirmed by testing:	.24 .1317(b)(4)			
a. Unknown serum with known A red cells	.24 .1317(b)(4)			
b. Unknown serum with known B red cells				
c. Results recorded	74.50 405.1316			
14. The reliability of each vial of reagent is tested each day of use with:	.24 .1317(b)(4)			
a. A known positive control	.24 .1317(b)(4)			
b. A known negative control				
c. Results recorded	74.50 405.1316			
15. The reliability of each vial of cells is tested each day of use with:	.24 .1317(b)(4)			
a. A known positive control	.24 .1317(b)(4)			
b. A known negative control				
c. Results recorded	74.50 405.1316			

continued

213

	CFR No.	Yes	No	NA	Comments—Identify by Number
HISTOCOMPATIBILITY 405.1317(b)(8)—*Continued*					
HISTOCOMPATIBILITY COMPATIBILITY TESTING 405.1317(b)(8)					
16. Compatibility testing of potential recipients and donors before transplantation is performed using the most reactive and most recent sera. Results recorded	.1317(b)(8) 74.50 405.1316				
17. HLA serological typing is performed employing ALL of the National Institute of Health Class I minimal standard antigens. Results recorded	.1317(b)(8) 74.50 405.1316				
INVESTIGATIVE STUDIES					
18. If the laboratory does investigative studies for the transfusion of leukocytes *or* platelets *or* of bone marrow transplantation the following procedures are performed:	405.1317(b)(8)				
a. Compatibility testing of potential recipients and donors before transplantation is performed using the most recent sera.	.1317(b)(8)				
b. Results recorded	74.50 405.1316				

		Reference
c.	HLA serological typing is performed employing ALL of the National Institute of Health Class I minimal standard antigens.	.1317(b)(8)
d.	Results recorded	74.50 405.1316

DISEASE ASSOCIATED STUDIES

		Reference
19.	If the laboratory does disease associated studies, the following procedures are performed:	.1317(b)(8)
a.	HLA serological typing for HLA-B27	.1317(b)(8)
b.	Results recorded	74.50 405.1316
c.	Special controls testing for the cross-reactivity of HLA-B27 concurrently with tests for HLA-B27	.1317(b)(8)
d.	Results recorded	74.50 405.1316

215

glossary

1. Accuracy. Deviation of an estimate from the true value.
2. Bias. The tendency to deviate from the true value caused by factors such as nonrandom sampling.
3. Blank. A solution containing all of the constituents of the test with the exception of the constituent being analyzed for.
4. Calibration. A quantitative measurement to ensure the accuracy of instruments.
5. Clinical Laboratory Improvement Act. An Act passed by Congress in 1967 to compel laboratories involved in interstate shipment of specimens to conform with acceptable standards of overall laboratory performance.
6. Coefficient of Variation. The standard deviation divided by the mean and expressed as a percent.
7. Confidence Limits. The high and low limits of a desired confidence interval.
8. Confirmation. The steps taken to ensure the proper operation of instruments and equipment.
9. Control Limits. Standard deviation based on the normal distribution of the total observation (68.26% ($\pm$1S), 95.45% ($\pm$2S), and 99.73% ($\pm$3S)).
10. Controls. Materials used (usually serum) to verify the desired conditions and mimic the actual specimen.
11. Degrees of Freedom. The number of variations possible among individual observations.
12. Gaussian Curve. A graphic representation of the distribution of values from the mean.
13. Median. Where as many cases exist above as below the line.
14. Mode. Value in a series which appears most frequently.
15. Outlier. Beyond acceptable limits. A value not relating to analytical variation; therefore, it is not to be considered in calculations.
16. Precision. Reproducibility percentage.
17. Preventive Maintenance. A program of periodic inspection and adjustment designed to alleviate breakdown of equipment and instruments.
18. Primary Standard. A certified standard.
19. Procedures Manual. A written set of instructions prepared by the laboratory and used to standardize testing procedures.
20. Quality Control. Techniques used to ensure the precision and accuracy of reagents, chemicals, media, techniques, and personnel.
21. Random. A condition which does not lend itself to predictive results.
22. Range. The difference between the highest and the lowest value.

23. Secondary Standards. Material used to calibrate. The lineage of the secondary standard may or may not be traceable to the primary standard.
24. Shelf-life. The date or time beyond which a reagent, control, or standard must not be used.
25. Shewhart Chart. A graphic representation of precision.
26. Standard Deviation. The square root of the average of the squared deviations from the arithmetic mean.
27. Standards. Materials used (usually certified) to adjust and control the accuracy of all parameters and allow the exact production of a previous attempt at standardizing.
28. Statistics. Those facts that can be stated as integer or real values.
29. Stock Cultures. Organisms that can be expected to perform in a reproducible manner and that conform to certain biochemical, morphological, and serological characteristics.
30. Warning Limits. Limits (usually ±2 standard deviations) on the control or Shewhart Chart.

bibliography

1. Moroney, M. J. 1951. Facts from Figures. Penguin Books, Ltd., Harmondsworth, England.
2. Shewhart, W. A. Industrial Quality Control. 1947 (July). 4:23.
3. Shewhart, W. A. 1931. Economic Control of Quality of Manufactured Product. Van Nostrand Co., Inc., New York.
4. Wooton, I. D. P., and King, E. J. 1953. Normal values for blood constituents: Interhospital differences. Lancet 1:470.
5. Halper, H. R., and Foster, H. S. 1976. Laboratory Regulation Manual. Aspen Systems Corporation, Germantown, Maryland.
6. Second Round Table on Quality Control in Clinical Microbiology. 1969. Published and Distributed by General Diagnostics Division of Warner-Lambert Pharmaceutical Company.
7. Davidsohn, I., and Henry, J. B. (eds.). 1974. Clinical Diagnosis by Laboratory Methods. 15th Ed. W. B. Saunders Company, Philadelphia.
8. Lennette, E., Spaulding, E., and Truant, J. (eds.). 1974. Manual of Clinical Microbiology. 2nd Ed. American Society for Microbiology, Washington, D.C.
9. Westlake, G. E., and Bennington, J. L. (eds.). 1972. Automation and Management in the Clinical Laboratory. University Park Press, Baltimore.
10. A preventative maintenance in the laboratory. 1970 (June). Laboratory Management, New York.
11. A guide on laboratory administration. 1976. U.S. Department of Health, Education and Welfare, Public Health Service. Center for Disease Control, Atlanta, Georgia.
12. Winstead, Martha. 1971. Instrument Check Systems. Lea and Febiger, Philadelphia.
13. Quality Control–Clinical Chemistry. 1973. 3rd Ed. U.S. Department of Health, Education and Welfare, Public Health Service, Center for Disease Control, Atlanta, Georgia.
14. Pfizer Diagnostic Technical Bulletin 3-b. 1972. VWR Scientific. Atlanta, Georgia.
15. Youden, W. J. Statistical techniques for collaborative tests. The Association of Official Analytical Chemists, Box 540, Benjamin Franklin Station, Washington, D.C. 20044.
16. Handbook for Analytical Quality Control in Water and Wastewater Laboratories. 1972 (June). Analytical Quality Control Laboratory. National Environmental Research Center, Cincinnati.
17. Dade Diagnostic. Dade Division, American Hospital Supply Corporation, P.O. Box 520672, Miami, Florida, 33152.
18. American Association of Blood Banks, Technical Methods and Procedures. 1970, 5th Ed. J.P. Lippincott Co., Philadelphia. p. 44.

19. American Association of Blood Banks, Quality Control in Blood Banking. 1973. 2nd Ed. J.P. Lippincott Co., Philadelphia.
20. Quality Control in the Blood Bank. 1973 (April). Ortho Diagnostics, Raritan, N.Y. 98869.
21. Bartlett, R. C. 1970. Quality control in clinical microbiology. Copyright 1970 by A. S. C. P.
22. Ellis, R. J. 1976. Manual of quality control procedures for microbiology laboratories. U.S. Department of Health, Education and Welfare, Public Health Service. Center for Disease Control, Atlanta, Georgia.
23. Methodology, Evaluation, and Quality Control. 1974. A Symposium sponsored by the American Society for Microbiology, May 12, 1974.
24. Glaser, L., Bosley, G., and Boring, J. 1971. A systematic program of quality control in clinical microbiology. Am. J. Clin. Path. 56: 379—383.
25. Bartlett, R. C. 1974. Medical Microbiology: Quality Cost and Clinical Relevance. Wiley & Sons, Inc., New York.
26. Cumitech. 3. Practical Quality Control Procedures for the Clinical Microbiology Laboratory. 1976 (September). American Society for Microbiology.
27. Manual for Quality Control Procedures for Microbiology Laboratories. 1976 (October). 2nd Ed. U.S. Department of Health, Education and Welfare. Center for Disease Control, Atlanta, Georgia.
28. Bauer, A. W., Kirby, W. M. M., Sherris, J. C., and Turck, M. 1966. Antibiotic susceptibility testing by a standardized single disc method. Am. J. Clin. Path. 45:493—496.
29. Biological Safety Cabinets. 1976 (July). U.S. Department of Health, Education and Welfare. Laboratory Consultation Branch, Center for Disease Control, Atlanta, Georgia.
30. Laboratory Procedures for the Diagnosis of Intestinal Parasites. 1975. U.S. Department of Health, Education and Welfare. DHEW Publication No. (CDC) 75-8282. GPO No. 017—023—00091—8. Center for Disease Control, Atlanta, Georgia.
31. Serological Tests for Syphilis. 1969. U.S. Public Health Service. PHS Publication No. 411. U.S. Government Printing Office, Washington, D.C.
32. A Guide to the Performance of the Standardized Diagnostic Complement Fixation Method and Adaption to Micro Test. 1969. 1st Ed. U.S. Department of Health, Education and Welfare. PHS No. 1228. Center for Disease Control, Atlanta, Georgia.

index